4WD TRAILS

SOUTHWEST COLORADO

Printed in the United States of America

Front cover photo: Gold Lake on Arrastra Gulch Trail

Copyright © 1999 Swagman Publishing, Inc. All rights reserved.

Publisher's Cataloging-in-Publication
(Provided by Quality Books, Inc.)

Massey, Peter, 1951-
    4WD trails. No. 1, Southwest Colorado / Peter
Massey and Jeanne Wilson.—1st ed.
      p. cm.
      Includes bibliographical references
      ISBN: 0-9665675-4-4

      1. Automotive travel—Colorado—Guidebooks.
2. Trails—Colorado—Guidebooks. 3. Automobiles—
Four-wheel drive. 4. Colorado—Guidebooks.
I. Wilson, Jeanne, 1960- II. Title.

GV1024.M37 1999   917.88'2
                QBI99-752

4WD TRAILS
SOUTHWEST COLORADO

PETER MASSEY
AND JEANNE WILSON

SWAGMAN
PUBLISHING

Acknowledgements

During the two years it has taken to research, write, and publish this book, people have helped us in many ways. We owe them all special thanks.

We would like to express gratitude to the staff at the U.S. Forest Service, the Denver Public Library, the Colorado Historical Society, and the various Chambers of Commerce throughout Colorado who have given us guidance in our research.

We would like to recognize especially the following for their major contributions to this endeavor:

Graphic Design and Maps: **Deborah Rust Design**
Copyediting: **Alice Levine**
Proofreading: **James Barnett**

Publisher's Note: Every effort has been taken to ensure that the information in this book is accurate at press time. Please visit our web site to advise us of any corrections that you identify. We also welcome recommendations for new 4WD trails or other suggestions to improve this book.

S W A G M A N
P U B L I S H I N G

Swagman Publishing, Inc.
P.O. Box 519, Castle Rock, CO 80104
Phone: 303-660-3307
Toll-free: 800-660-5107
Fax: 303-688-4388
www.4wdbooks.com

Contents

Using This Book

Route Planning

The regional map on page 16 provides an overview of the trails in this book. Each 4WD trail is highlighted, as are major highways and towns, which makes it possible to relate the start and end points of every 4WD trail in this book to nearby roads and trails.

By referring to the map you can plan your overall route to utilize as many 4WD trails as possible. Checking the difficulty rating and time required for each trail allows you to finalize your plans.

Difficulty Ratings

We utilize a point system to indicate the difficulty of each trail. Any such system is subjective and is dependent on the driver's experience level and the current road conditions.

We have rated the 4WD trails in this book on a scale of 1 to 10, 1 being passable for a normal passenger vehicle in good conditions and 10 requiring a heavily modified vehicle and an experienced driver who is willing to expect vehicle damage. Because this book is designed for owners of unmodified 4WD vehicles whom we assume do not want to risk damage to their vehicles, nearly all the trails are rated 5 or lower.

This is not to say that all the trails in this book are easy. We strongly recommend that inexperienced drivers not tackle any 4- or 5-rated trails before undertaking a number of the lower-rated ones, so that they can gauge their skill level and prepare for the difficulty of the higher-rated trails.

In assessing the trails, we assume good road conditions (dry road surface, good visibility, and so on). Our ratings are based on the following factors:

■ obstacles such as rocks, mud, ruts, and stream crossings
■ the stability of the road surface
■ the width of the road and the vehicle clearance between trees or rocks
■ the steepness of the road
■ the margin of error (for example, a very high, open shelf road would be rated more difficult even if it was not very steep and had a stable surface)

The following is a guide to the ratings. As a rule only one of the criteria need to be met for the road to get a higher rating:

Rating 1: Graded dirt but suitable for a normal passenger vehicle. Gentle grades; fairly wide; very shallow water crossings (if any).

Rating 2: Road surface rarely or not maintained. Dirt road better suited to a high-clearance vehicle but passable in a normal passenger car; fairly wide, passing not a concern; mud not a concern under normal weather conditions.

Rating 3: High-clearance 4WD preferred. Rough road surface to be expected; mud possible but easily passable; rocks up to six inches in diameter; loose surface possible; shelf road but wide enough for passing or with adequate pull-offs.

Rating 4: High-clearance 4WD recommended. Rough road surface with rocks larger than six inches possible, but a reasonable driving line available; mud possible but passable; stream crossings less than fifteen inches deep; substantial sections of single-lane shelf road possible; moderate grades; moderately loose surface possible.

Rating 5: High-clearance 4WD required. Rough, rutted surface; rocks up to nine inches possible; mud may be impassable for inexperienced drivers; stream crossings up to twenty-four inches deep; sections may be steep enough to cause traction problems; very narrow shelf road with steep drop-offs should be expected; tight clearance between rocks or trees possible.

Rating 6: Experienced four-wheel drivers only. Potentially dangerous; large rocks, ruts, or terraces may need to be negotiated; steep slopes, loose surface, and/or very narrow vehicle clearance; stream crossings at least twenty-four inches deep, and/or unstable stream bottom, or difficult access; very narrow shelf road with steep drop-offs and challenging road surfaces to be expected.

Rating 7: Skilled, experienced four-wheel drivers only. Very challenging sections; very steep sections likely; loose surface, large rocks, deep ruts, and tight clearance expected; mud likely to necessitate winching.

Rating 8 to 10: Stock vehicles are likely to be damaged and may find the trail impassable. Well beyond the scope of this book.

Scenic Ratings

If rating the degree of difficulty is subjective, rating scenic beauty is guaranteed to lead to arguments—especially in Colorado, a stunningly beautiful state. However, we have tried to give some guide to the relative scenic quality of the various trails. The ratings are based on a scale of 1 to 10, with 10 being the most scenic.

Estimated Driving Times

In calculating driving times, we have not allowed for stops. Actual driving time may be considerably longer than indicated, depending on the number and duration of stops. Add more time if you prefer to drive more slowly than good conditions allow.

As with the distance cited for each trail, the time given for trails that dead-end is for travel one-way. The time that should be allowed for the overall trip, including the return to the start, may be more than double that indicated. However, with the

knowledge of the trail that has been gained going in, you may find that the return is usually completed more quickly.

Current Road Conditions

All the 4WD trails described in this book may be impassable in poor weather conditions. For each trail, we have provided a phone number for obtaining current information about conditions.

Abbreviations

The route directions provided for the 4WD trails in this book use a series of abbreviations.

SO	Continue straight on
TL	Turn left
TR	Turn right
BL	Bear left
BR	Bear right
UT	U-turn

Using Route Directions

To help you stay on track, we have described and pinpointed (by odometer reading) nearly every significant feature along the route (intersections, streams, gates, cattle guards, and so on) and have provided directions to follow from these landmarks. Odometer readings will vary from vehicle to vehicle, but you will soon learn to allow for slight variations.

If you diverge from the route, zero your trip meter upon your return and continue the route, making the necessary adjustment to the point-to-point odometer directions. We have regularly reset the odometer readings in the directions, so you won't have to recalculate for too long. Route directions include cross-references whenever the route crosses another 4WD trail included in this book, which allows easy change of route or destination. Directions for traveling the 4WD trails in reverse are printed in orange. When traveling in reverse, read from the bottom of the table and work up.

Latitude and longitude readings are provided periodically to facilitate the use of a Global Positioning System (GPS) receiver.

These readings may also assist in finding your location on your maps. The GPS coordinates were taken using the NAD 1927 datum and are in the format dd°mm.mmm'. When loading coordinates into your GPS receiver, you may wish to include only one decimal place because in Colorado, the third decimal place equals only about two yards and the second less than twenty yards.

Map References

We recommend that you supplement the information in this book with more-detailed maps. Each trail in this book refers to various sheet maps and road atlases that provide the detail necessary to navigate and identify accurately your location. Typically, the following five references are given:

■ U.S. Forest Service Maps—Scale 1:126,720

■ U.S. Geological Survey County Series Maps—Scale 1:50,000

■ *The Roads of Colorado,* 1st ed. (Fredericksburg, Texas: Shearer Publishing, 1996)—Scale 1:158,400

■ *Colorado Atlas & Gazetteer,* 2nd ed. (Freeport, Maine: DeLorme Mapping, 1995)—Scale 1:160,000 and 1:320,000

■ *Trails Illustrated* topo maps; National Geographic maps—Various scales, but all contain good detail

We recommend the *Trails Illustrated* maps. They are reliable, easy to read, and printed on nearly indestructible plastic "paper." However, the series does not cover all the 4WD trails described in this book.

If *Trails Illustrated* maps are not available, we recommend the U.S. Geological Survey County Series Maps. These show the necessary detail without being too detailed. Their main weakness is that some are out of date and do not show the 4WD trails accurately.

The two atlases are reasonably priced and include maps of the entire state. Although the atlases do not give much information for each 4WD trail beyond what we have provided, they are helpful if you wish to explore side roads. Of the two, we prefer *The Roads of Colorado.*

U.S. Forest Service maps lack the detail of the other sheet maps and, in our experience, are also out of date occasionally. They have the advantage of covering a broad area. These maps are most useful for the longer trails.

For those who want to navigate with the assistance of a portable computer, Maptech publishes a particularly good series of maps on CD-ROM. These are based on the U.S. Geological Survey 7.5° Series Maps—Scale 1:24,000, but they can be viewed on four scales. The 1:100,000-scale series are also included. These maps offer many advantages over normal maps:

■ GPS coordinates for any location can be found, which can then be loaded into your GPS receiver. Conversely, if you know your GPS coordinates, your location on the map can be pinpointed instantly.

■ Towns, rivers, passes, mountains, and many other sites are indexed by name so that they can be located quickly.

■ 4WD trails can be marked and profiled for elevation change and distance from point to point.

■ Customized maps can be printed out.

To cover the entire state of Colorado requires 8 CD ROMs, which is expensive; however, the CD ROMs can be purchased individually.

All these maps should be available through good map stores. The CD ROMs are available directly from Maptech (800-627-7236 or on the Internet at www.maptech.com).

Driving Off-Highway

Four-wheel driving involves special road rules and techniques. This section is provided as an introduction for 4WD beginners.

4WD Road Rules

To help ensure that these trails remain open and available for all four-wheel drivers to enjoy, it is important to minimize your impact on the environment and not be a safety risk to yourself or anyone else. Remember that the 4WD clubs in Colorado fight a constant battle with the U.S. Forest Service to retain access.

The fundamental rule when traversing the 4WD trails described in this book is to use common sense. In addition, special road rules for 4WD trails apply.

■ Vehicles traveling uphill have the right of way.

■ If you are moving more slowly than the vehicle behind you, pull over to let the other vehicle by.

■ Park out of the way in a safe place. Set the parking brake—don't rely on leaving the transmission in park. Manual transmissions should be left in the lowest gear.

In addition to these rules, we offer the following advice to four-wheel drivers.

■ Size up the situation in advance.

■ Be careful. Take your time.

■ Maintain smooth, steady power and momentum.

■ Engage 4WD and low-range before you get into a tight situation.

■ Steer toward high spots and try to put the wheel over large rocks.

■ Straddle ruts.

■ Use gears rather than only the brakes to hold the vehicle when driving downhill. On very steep slopes, chock the wheels when you park your vehicle.

■ Watch for logging and mining trucks.

■ Wear your seat belt and ensure that all luggage, especially heavy items such as toolboxes or coolers, is secured. Heavy items should be secured by ratchet tie-down straps rather than elastic-type straps, which are not strong enough to hold heavy items if the vehicle rolls.

Tread Lightly!

Remember the rules of the Tread Lightly!® program.

■ Become informed. Obtain maps, regulations, and other information from the U.S. Forest Service or from other public land agencies. Learn the rules and follow them.

■ Resist the urge to pioneer a new road or trail or to cut across a switchback. Stay on constructed tracks and avoid running over young trees, shrubs, and grasses, damaging or killing them. Don't drive across alpine tundra; this fragile environment may take years to recover.

■ Stay off soft, wet roads and 4WD trails readily torn up by vehicles. Repairing the damage is expensive.

■ Travel around meadows, steep hillsides, stream banks, and lake shores that are easily scarred by churning wheels.

■ Stay away from wild animals that are rearing young or suffering from a food shortage.

■ Obey gate closures and regulatory signs.

■ Preserve America's heritage by not disturbing old mining camps, ghost towns, or other historical features.

■ Carry out all rubbish.

■ Stay out of designated wilderness areas. They are closed to all vehicles. Know where the boundaries are.

■ Get permission to cross private land. Leave livestock alone. Respect landowners' rights.

Special Four-Wheel Driving Techniques

Certain obstacles are likely to be encountered on Colorado's 4WD trails. The following provides an introduction to the techniques required for dealing with the most common situations.

Rocks. Tire selection is important because sharp rocks are often encountered on Colorado mountain 4WD trails. Select a multiple-ply, tough sidewall, light-truck tire with a large-lug tread.

As you approach a rocky stretch, get into 4WD low range to give you maximum slow-speed control. Speed is rarely necessary since traction on a rocky surface is usually good. Plan ahead and select the line you wish to take. If the rock appears to be larger than the clearance of your vehicle, don't try to straddle it. Check to see that it is not higher than the frame of your vehicle once you get a wheel over it. Put a wheel up to the rock and slowly climb it; then gently drop over the other side, using the brake to ensure a smooth landing. Bouncing the car over rocks increases the likelihood of damage, as the suspension compressing reduces the clearance. Running boards also significantly reduce your clearance in this respect.

Steep Uphill Grades. Consider walking the trail to ensure that it is passable, especially if it is clear that backtracking is going to be a problem.

Select 4WD low range to ensure that you have adequate power to pull up the hill. If the wheels begin to lose traction, try turning the steering wheel gently from side to side to give the wheels a chance to regain traction.

If you lose momentum, but the car is not in danger of sliding, use the foot brake, switch off the ignition, leave the vehicle in gear (if manual transmission) or park (if automatic), engage the parking brake, and get out to examine the situation. See if you can remove any obstacles, and figure out the line you need to take. Reversing a couple of yards and starting again may allow you to get better traction and momentum.

If you decide a stretch of road is impassably steep, back down the trail. Trying to turn the vehicle around is extremely dangerous and very likely to cause it to roll over.

Steep Downhill Grades. Again, consider walking the trail to ensure that it is passable, especially if it is clear that backtracking is going to be a problem.

Select 4WD low range, in first gear, to maximize braking assistance from the engine. If the surface is loose and you are losing traction, change up to second or third gear. Do not use the brakes if you can avoid it, but don't let the vehicle's speed get out of control. Feather (lightly pump) the brakes if you slip under braking.

Travel very slowly over rock ledges or ruts. Attempt to tackle these diagonally, letting one wheel down at a time.

If the vehicle begins to slide around at the back, gently apply the throttle and correct the steering. If the rear of the vehicle starts to slide sideways, do not apply the brakes.

Mud. Muddy trails are easily damaged, so they should be avoided if possible. If you do need to traverse a section of mud, your success will depend heavily on whether you have open-lugged mud tires or chains.

Thick mud fills the tighter tread that is on normal tires, leaving the tire with no more grip than if it were bald. If the muddy stretch is only a few yards long, the momentum of your vehicle may allow you to get through regardless.

If the muddy track is very steep, either uphill or downhill, do not attempt it. Your vehicle is very likely to skid in such conditions and the vehicle may roll or slip off the edge of the road.

When crossing mud:

■ Avoid making detours off existing tracks, so that environmental damage is minimized.

■ Check to see that the mud has a reasonably firm base (tackling deep mud is definitely not recommended unless you have a vehicle-mounted winch—and even then, be cautious because the winch may not get you out).

■ Check to see that no ruts are too deep for the ground clearance of your vehicle.

Having decided that you can get through and having selected the best route, use the following techniques:

■ Select 4WD low range and a suitable gear; momentum is the key to success, so use a high enough gear to build up sufficient speed.

■ Avoid accelerating heavily, so as to minimize wheel spinning and provide maximum traction.

■ Follow existing wheel ruts, unless they are too deep for the clearance of your vehicle.

■ Correct slides by turning the steering wheel in the direction that the rear wheels are skidding, but don't be too aggressive with the amount you correct your steering.

■ If the vehicle comes to a stop, don't continue to accelerate, as you will only spin your wheels and dig yourself into a rut. Try backing out and having another go.

Stream Crossings. By crossing a stream that is too deep, drivers risk far more than water flowing in and ruining the interior of their vehicles. Water sucked into the engine's air intake will seriously damage the engine. Likewise, water that seeps into the air vent on the transmission or differential will mix with the lubricant and may lead to serious problems. Water that gets into the interior of modern vehicles may damage the computerized vehicle management system. Even worse than damage to a vehicle is the possibility that deep or fast flowing water could easily carry a vehicle downstream and may endanger the lives of the occupants.

The manual for some 4WDs will say what fording depth the vehicle can negotiate safely. If your vehicle's owner's manual doesn't include this information, your local dealer may be able to assist. If you don't know, then you should try to avoid crossing through water that is more than a foot or so deep.

The first rule for crossing a stream is to know what you are getting into. You need to ascertain how deep the water is, make sure that there are no large rocks or holes and that the bottom is solid enough to avoid getting the vehicle bogged, and see that the entry and exit points are negotiable. This assessment may take some time and you may get wet, but to cross a stream without first properly evaluating the situation is to take a great risk.

The secret to water crossings is to keep moving, but not to move too quickly. In shallow water (where the surface of the water is below the bumper), your primary concern is to safely negotiate the bottom of the stream, avoiding any rock damage and maintaining momentum if there is a danger of getting stuck or slipping on the exit.

In deeper water (between eighteen and thirty inches deep), the objective is to create a small bow wave in front of the moving vehicle. This requires a speed that is approximately walking pace. The bow wave reduces the depth of the water around the engine compartment. If the water's surface reaches your tailpipe, select a gear that will maintain moderate engine revs to avoid water backing up into the exhaust; do not change gears midstream.

Crossing water deeper than thirty inches requires more extensive preparation of the vehicle and should be attempted only by experienced drivers.

Snow. The trails in this book are nearly all closed until the snow has melted or been bulldozed. Therefore, the only snow conditions that you are likely to encounter are an occasional snowdrift that has not yet melted or fresh snow from an unexpected storm. Getting through such conditions depends on the depth of the snow, its consistency, the stability of the underlying surface, and your vehicle.

If the snow is no deeper than about nine inches and there is solid ground beneath it, it should not pose a problem. In deeper snow that seems solid enough to support your vehicle, be extremely cautious: If you break through a drift, you are likely to be stuck, and if conditions are bad, you may have a long wait.

The tires you use for off-highway driving, with a wide tread pattern, are probably suitable for these snow conditions. Nonetheless, it is wise to carry chains (preferably for all four wheels) and even wiser to travel with a vehicle-mounted winch.

It is important to remember how quickly the weather can change in the Colorado high country, even in summer. Pack clothes and other items to ensure your survival if you are caught in a sudden storm.

Sand. As with most off-highway situations, your tires will affect your ability to cross sand. It is difficult to tell how well a particular tire will handle in sand just by looking at it, so be guided by the manufacturer and your dealer.

The key to driving in soft sand is floatation, which is achieved by a combination of low tire pressure and momentum. Before crossing a stretch of sand, you should start by reducing your tire pressure to between fifteen and twenty pounds. If necessary, you can safely go to as low as twelve pounds. As you cross the sand, maintain momentum so that your vehicle rides on the top of soft sand without digging in or stalling. This may require plenty of engine power.

Air the tires back up as soon as you are out of the sand to avoid damage to the tires and the rims. Airing back up requires a high-quality air compressor. Even then, it is a slow process.

The only trail in this book that may necessitate lowering the tire pressure for sand is the Medano Pass road, which ends in the Great Sand Dunes National Monument. A refill station at the national monument is open in the peak season, which may mean that if you air down on this trail, you can avoid buying a portable compressor.

Vehicle Recovery Methods

You are sure to get stuck sooner or later. The following techniques will help you get going. The most suitable method will depend on the equipment available and the situation you are in—whether you are stuck in sand, mud, or snow, or high-centered, or unable to negotiate a hill.

Towing. Use a strong nylon yank strap, twenty to thirty feet long, two to three inches wide, rated to at least 20,000 pounds, and preferably with looped ends. This type of strap will stretch 15 to 25 percent, and the elasticity will assist in extracting the vehicle.

Attach the strap to a frame-mounted tow hook. Ensure that the driver of the stuck vehicle is ready, take up all but about six feet of slack, and then move the towing vehicle away at a moderate speed (in most circumstances this means using 4WD low range in second gear) so that the elasticity of the strap is employed in the way it is meant to be. Don't take off like a bat out of hell or you risk breaking the strap or damaging a vehicle.

Never join two yank straps together with a shackle. If one strap breaks, the shackle will become a lethal missile aimed at one of the vehicles (and anyone inside). For the same reason, never attach a yank strap to the tow ball on either vehicle.

Jacking. Jacking the vehicle may allow you to pack under the wheel (with rocks, dirt, or logs) or use your shovel to remove an obstacle. However, the standard vehicle jack is unlikely to be of as much assistance as a high-lift jack. We highly recommend purchasing a good high-lift jack as a basic accessory if you decide that you are going to do a lot of serious, off-highway, four-wheel driving.

Tire Chains. Tire chains can be of assistance in mud and snow. Link-type chains provide much more grip than cable-type chains. There are also dedicated mud chains with larger, heavier links than normal snow chains.

It is best to have chains fitted on all four wheels. However, this may not be possible since some vehicles lack sufficient clearance between the wheel and the fender. Remove chains from the front wheels as soon as practicable to avoid undue strain on the vehicle.

Be aware that it is more difficult to fit the chains after you are stuck; if at all possible try to predict their need and have them on the vehicle before trouble arises.

Winching. Most people using this book will not have a winch. But if you get serious about four-wheel driving, this is probably the first major accessory you will consider buying.

Under normal circumstances, a winch would be warranted only for the more difficult 4WD trails in this book. Having a winch is certainly comforting when you see a difficult section of road ahead and have to decide whether to risk it or turn back. Major obstacles can appear when you least expect them, even on trails that are otherwise easy.

A winch is not a panacea to all your recovery problems. Winching depends on the availability of a good anchor point, and an electric winch may not work if it is submerged in a stream. Despite these constraints, no accessory is more useful than a high-quality, powerful winch when you get into a difficult situation.

If you acquire a winch, learn to use it properly; take the time to study your owner's manual. Incorrect operation can be extremely dangerous and may cause damage to the winch or to trees, which are the most common anchors.

Navigation by the Global Positioning System (GPS)

Although this book is designed so that each trail can be navigated by simply following the detailed directions provided, nothing makes navigation easier than a GPS receiver.

The Global Positioning System (GPS)

consists of a network of twenty-four satellites, nearly thirteen thousand miles in space, in six different orbital paths. The satellites are constantly moving, making two complete orbits around the earth every twenty-four hours at about 8,500 miles per hour. Each satellite is constantly transmitting data, including its identification number, its operational health, and the date and time. It also transmits its location and the location of every other satellite in the network.

By comparing the time a signal was transmitted to the time it is received, a GPS receiver calculates how far away each satellite is. With a sufficient number of signals, the receiver can then triangulate its location. With three or more satellites, the receiver can determine latitude and longitude coordinates. With four or more, it can calculate altitude. By constantly making these calculations, it can calculate speed and direction.

The U.S. military uses the system to provide positions accurate to within half an inch. However, civilian receivers are less sophisticated and are deliberately fed slightly erroneous information in order to effectively deny military applications to hostile countries or terrorists. Because of this degradation of the signal, which is called Selective Availability (SA), the common civilian receivers have an accuracy of twenty to seventy-five yards.

A GPS receiver offers the four-wheel driver numerous benefits.

■ You can track to any point for which you know the longitude and latitude coordinates with no chance of heading in the wrong direction or getting lost. Most receivers provide an extremely easy-to-understand graphic display to keep you on track.

■ It works in all weather conditions.

■ It automatically records your route for easy backtracking.

■ You can record and name any location, so that you can relocate it with ease. This may include your campsite, a fishing spot, or even a silver mine you discover!

■ It displays your position, allowing you to pinpoint your location on a map.

■ By interfacing the GPS receiver directly to a portable computer, you can monitor and record your location as you travel (using the appropriate map software) or print the route you took.

GPS receivers have come down in price considerably in the past few years and are rapidly becoming indispensable navigational tools. Many higher-priced cars now offer integrated GPS receivers; and within the next few years, receivers will become available on most models.

Battery-powered, hand-held units that meet the needs of off-highway driving currently range from less than $100 to a little over $300 and continue to come down in price. Some high-end units feature maps that are incorporated in the display, either from a built-in database or from interchangeable memory cards. However, none of these maps currently include 4WD trails in their database.

If you are considering purchasing a GPS unit, look for the following features:

■ Price. The very cheapest units are likely outdated and very limited in their display features. Expect to pay $125 to $300.

■ The number of channels, which means the number of satellites that the unit tracks concurrently. Many older units have only one channel that switches from one satellite to another to collect the required information. Modern units have up to twelve channels, which are each dedicated to tracking one satellite. A greater number of channels provides greater accuracy, faster start-up (because the unit can acquire the initial data it needs much more rapidly), and better reception under difficult conditions (for example, if you are in a deep canyon or in dense foliage).

■ The number of routes and the number of sites (or "waypoints") per route that can be stored in memory. For off-highway use, it is important to be able to store many waypoints so that you do not have to load coordinates into the machine as frequently. Having sufficient memory also ensures that you can automatically store your location without fear that you will run out of memory.

■ It is also important that the machine can store numerous routes. GPS receivers enable you to combine waypoints to form a route, greatly simplifying navigation. As you reach each waypoint, the machine automatically swaps to the next one and directs you there.

■ The better units store up to five hundred waypoints and twenty reversible routes of up to thirty waypoints each. Also consider the number of characters a GPS receiver allows you to use in naming waypoints. When you try to recall a waypoint, you may have difficulty recognizing names restricted to only a few characters.

■ Automatic route storing. Most units automatically store your route as you go along and enable you to display it in reverse to make backtracking easy.

■ The display. Compare graphic displays. Some are much easier to decipher or offer more alternative displays.

■ The controls. Because GPS receivers have many functions, they need to have good, simple controls.

■ Vehicle mounting. To be useful, the unit needs to be located so that it can be read easily by both the driver and the navigator. Check that the unit can be conveniently located in your vehicle. Units have different shapes and mounting systems.

■ Position-format options. Maps use different grids; you should be able to display the same format on your GPS unit as on the map you are using, so that cross-referencing is simplified. There are a number of formats for latitude and longitude, as well as the UTM (Universal Transverse Mercator) grid, which is used on some maps.

After you have selected a unit, a number of optional extras are also worth considering:

■ A cigarette lighter adapter. Important because GPS units eat batteries!

■ A vehicle-mounted antenna, which will improve reception under difficult conditions. (The GPS unit can only "see" though the windows of your vehicle; it cannot monitor satellites through a metal roof.) Having a vehicle-mounted antenna also means that you do not have to consider reception when locating the receiver in your vehicle.

■ An in-car mounting system. If you are going to do a lot of touring using the GPS, you may want to attach a bracket on the dash rather than relying on a velcro mount.

■ A computer-link cable. Data from your receiver can be downloaded to your PC; or, if you have a laptop computer, you can monitor your route as you go along, using one of a number of inexpensive map software products on the market.

We used a Garmin 45 receiver to take the GPS positions in this book. This unit is now outdated, but it has served us well for the past five years in our travels throughout the United States and around the world.

Trails in the Southwest Region

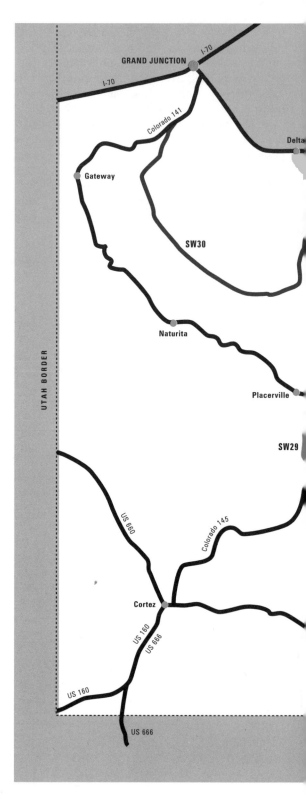

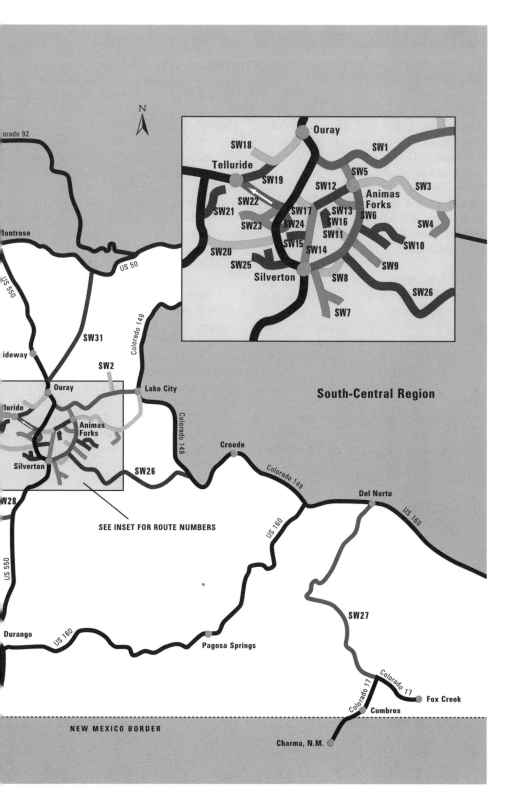

N

orado 92

Ouray

SW18

SW1

Telluride

SW5

SW19

SW12

SW3

SW22

Animas
Forks

Montrose

SW21

SW17

SW13

SW6

SW4

SW23

SW24

SW16

US 50

SW11

SW15

SW10

SW20

SW14

US 550

Colorado 149

SW25

SW9

Silverton

SW8

SW26

SW31

SW7

SW2

ideway

Ouray

Lake City

South-Central Region

luride

Colorado 149

Animas
Forks

Creede

Colorado 149

Silverton

Colorado 149

Del Norte

SW26

US 160

W28

US 160

SEE INSET FOR ROUTE NUMBERS

US 550

SW27

Durango

US 160

Pagosa Springs

Colorado 17

Colorado 17

Fox Creek

Colorado 17

NEW MEXICO BORDER

Cumbres

Charma, N.M.

Engineer Pass Trail

STARTING POINT Ouray
FINISHING POINT Lake City—Intersection with
Southwest #3: Cinnamon Pass Trail
TOTAL MILEAGE 31.0 miles
UNPAVED MILEAGE 27.2 miles
DRIVING TIME 3 hours
ROUTE ELEVATION 8,932 to 12,750 feet
USUALLY OPEN Mid-June to early October
DIFFICULTY RATING 4
SCENIC RATING 10

Special Attractions

- Part of the historic Alpine Loop, with many famous mining sites.
- Driving through the twenty-foot deep channel in the snow early in the season.
- Spectacular Rocky Mountain scenery.
- Whitmore Falls.

History

Six years before building the Million Dollar Highway between Ouray and Silverton, Otto Mears extended his toll road from Saguache to Lake City and through to Animas Forks, via Engineer Pass. Mears's network of toll roads continued south to Eureka and Silverton and north to Mineral Point, Poughkeepsie, and Ouray.

From its completion in August 1877, this road was an important stagecoach route and the principal freight route for the wagons and mule trains that hauled supplies and ore between all the main mining camps in the area and Saguache, which was the closest major supply center. Within three years, the route had daily stages run by the Rocky Mountain Stage and Express Company.

The Engineer Pass 4WD trail passes the sites of some of the major mining camps that were established in the area. The turnoff to the first, Poughkeepsie, is located two and one-half miles from the start of the trail. This town sat at an altitude of 11,650 feet about seven miles south of Ouray; its remote location and the poor quality of the roads leading to it hindered development. The winters were so harsh that miners could work only two or three months of the year. Despite the hardships Poughkeepsie residents had to endure, the town was surprisingly well planned. It had a post office established in 1880, a newspaper called the *Poughkeepsie Telegraph*, stores, restaurants, saloons, and other businesses. Miners usually sent ore to Lake City or Silverton via rough roads by burro. Transporting the ore in this manner was so difficult and expensive that eventually mine owners decided it wasn't worth it and ceased operations. No buildings from the town remain.

Mineral Point mining camp was located about one and three-quarters of a mile southwest of Engineer Pass, at an altitude of 11,500 feet. The camp was founded by prospectors Abe Burrows and Charles McIntyre in 1873. To generate interest in the camp, promoters of Mineral Point circulated far-fetched advertisements with unrealistic claims and pictures to raise capital. One advertisement depicted a steamship running up the Animas River and streetcars running from Mineral Point to Animas Forks!

In truth, only very mediocre transportation was available, and miners had to use cumbersome wagons or burros to transport their ore. Most was sent either to Silverton via Animas Forks or to Lake City. Because of

Empire Chief Mill

Palmetto Gulch cabin

the inhospitable winters, the lack of transportation, and the silver crash of 1893, by the mid-1890s Mineral Point was on its way to becoming a ghost camp.

Just beyond Engineer Pass is the site of Engineer City, established around 1874 when H. A. Woods staked the first claim in the area and named it the Annie Woods Lode. By 1875, the population of prospectors grew to about four hundred. For a short time, Engineer City prided itself on being the largest city in the state without a saloon. The prospectors were simply too busy looking for silver to spend time in a bar. In 1882, the Frank Hough Mine was discovered. A camp of about fifty men operated it in American Flats on the eastern side of Engineer Mountain. It was closed in 1900, and the ruins of the mine remain.

Rose's Cabin was once a lively inn offering food, lodging, and entertainment to miners and travelers. Corydon Rose was one of the first pioneers to explore the San Juans after a treaty was signed with the Utes in 1873. Rose decided to build an inn to serve the area, locating it about halfway between Ouray and Lake City to provide a convenient stopover for travelers along the route.

The area around the cabin began to grow in population as miners settled there. They built cabins nearby and worked mines in the surrounding hills. It is estimated that about fifty people settled in the vicinity. Rose's Cabin served the community as its local bar, restaurant, hotel, general store, and post office. Rose kept sixty burros in a stable to ship supplies to the miners and carry their ore down to his cabin. The cabin was the hive of activity in the region. Only a few traces of the cabin remain. The structure still standing is the old stable; the cabin was situated to the left.

Capitol City was established about ten miles west of Lake City after rich silver discoveries in 1877 brought prospectors to the area. The town of Galena City began as a tent city, but the tents were soon replaced by more permanent structures. George S. Lee, a miner

THE UTE AND CHIEF OURAY

The vast area west of the Front Range was almost entirely controlled by various bands of Ute, who had lived there for approximately ten thousand years, longer than any other tribe lived within the future boundaries of Colorado. Ute domination of the entire area west of the eastern slope of the Rockies did not alter in the period leading up to the establishment of the Colorado Territory in 1861. In 1859, the Pikes Peak gold rush had erupted, and thousands of white prospectors and settlers poured across the eastern plains of Colorado, which were controlled by the Cheyenne and Arapaho. From his appointment in 1862, Governor Evans sought to open up eastern Colorado to these white settlers; but the two tribes refused to sell their lands and move to reservations. Evans decided to force the issue through what became known as the Cheyenne-Arapaho War, or the Colorado War, of 1864–1865.

During this period, the Ute maintained an uneasy peace with the whites who were slowly encroaching on their lands. The initial fur trapping and prospecting had not greatly affected the Ute way of life, but numerous gold discoveries in central Colorado, from 1858 to 1860, led to greater incursions of white settlers into Ute territory.

In 1868, in response to the influx of miners and continued pressure for land to settle, a treaty known as the Kit Carson Treaty was negotiated by Chief Ouray, whereby the Ute gave up their land in the central Rockies and San Luis Valley and agreed to be settled on 16 million acres of land in western Colorado. The Colorado territory that the Ute retained was a rectangle that sat against the western and southern borders of the state, with its eastern border reaching almost to where Gunnison and Steamboat Springs are presently located, and its northern border located just south of the Yampa River. Two agencies, the White River Agency and the Los Pinos Agency, were established in 1869 to maintain the reservation and to distribute the promised $50,000 worth of supplies to the Ute every year.

Chief Ouray with Otto Mears in 1880

Early prospecting efforts into the San Juan Mountains, the heartland of the Uncompahgre Ute, were slowed not so much by the Kit Carson Treaty or the fearsome reputation of the Ute, but by the lack of early success in finding gold and the intrusion

with grand plans, had the town's name changed to Capitol City because he was certain that Colorado would move its capital to the San Juan Mountains, and he would live in the governor's mansion. To aid in the construction of Capitol City, Lee built a sawmill and planing mill. He also erected the Henson Creek Smelter, one mile below the town, to process ore from the many mines nearby

A town site of two hundred acres was laid out; a schoolhouse was built, athough the population never exceeded four hundred and there were only a handful of students. Lee built himself a large and elegant house at the edge of

town to be the governor's mansion, where he and his wife entertained lavishly. Their home even had a ballroom and orchestra pit. Bricks imported from Pueblo were estimated to have cost a dollar apiece! However, Lee's efforts did not bear fruit: Capitol City never even became the county seat.

About four miles before reaching Lake City the road goes through the town of Henson, a mining camp that grew up around the Ute-Ulay Mine. In 1871, Harry Henson discovered the mine but the land belonged to the Indians, who did not take kindly to white trespassers. Henson was of the Civil War. However, in the early 1870s, pressure from mining increased dramatically. Discoveries at Henson and in the Animas River Valley and prospecting in many other areas led to yet another treaty and further loss of land by the Ute. The Brunot Treaty, signed by Chief Ouray and other Ute chiefs in Washington in 1873, ceded the San Juan region from their reservation. When Colorado achieved statehood in 1876, the miners and settlers again sought to have the treaties renegotiated. The political slogan became "The Utes Must Go."

Chief Ouray recognized the futility of resisting white expansion but was unable to control all the bands of Ute. The White River Ute especially resented the Brunot Treaty, which Ouray had been instrumental in negotiating. Nathan C. Meeker was appointed the Indian agent of the White River Ute in 1878. He was convinced that for their own good the Ute should give up hunting for agriculture and the Christian religion. When Meeker plowed the grazing land used by the Ute horses, a medicine man, Chief Johnson, attacked him. In response to this attack, in September 1879, federal officials sent in 150 troops under the command of Major Thomas Thornburgh.

Chief Douglas and Chief Jack considered the calling of troops an act of war. Ute scouts warned the army not to enter reservation lands, which was prohibited by treaty agreement. The soldiers continued and were attacked. Major Thornburgh was killed and his troops besieged until Captain Francis S. Dodge and his cavalry of "Buffalo Soldiers" rescued them.

At the agency, the Ute burned the agency buildings, killed Meeker and the other white men, and took Meeker's daughter, his wife, and another woman into the mountains and held them captive for twenty-three days. Ouray acted swiftly to negotiate the release of the white women, but the political storm that ensued could not save the Ute from losing their reservation lands. After weeks of testimony before congressional committees in Washington, the Washington Treaty was signed in 1880 by Chiefs Ouray, Shavano, Antero, and others. It was necessary for three-quarters of the Ute males to sign this new treaty for it to come into effect. Otto Mears was appointed commissioner to secure the signatures. In August 1880, before all the signatures were obtained, Ouray died at the age of forty-six. Within a year, all the Ute were removed to reservations in Utah and southwestern Colorado.

Land developers and settlers gathered in Gunnison in the summer of 1881, waiting for the last of the Ute to vacate the old reservation, which they did on September 7, 1881. In 1882, Congress declared the Ute lands public and open for filing, but many settlers had already moved in and laid out towns.

unable to develop the property until well after the Brunot Treaty of 1873, as violence with the Indians continued for several years. White settlers clashed with the native Indians near Lake City as late as 1879.

There was also a long, bitter, and violent miners' strike in Henson. Reportedly, the strike started because the mine owners insisted that all single men board at the company boardinghouse. To protest, miners went on strike. When the owners hired non-union labor to replace the striking miners, fights erupted and some scabs were run out of town. The volatility of the situation prompted the governor of Colorado to send four companies of cavalry and two companies of infantry to settle the dispute. The dispute eventually went to trial, and all the miners were forced to leave camp.

Henson's post office, established in May 1883, was closed in November 1913. The buildings still standing in Henson are privately owned, and many are still in use.

Description

This route commences south from Ouray on the Million Dollar Highway, US 550.

If you wish to avoid the hardest section

of the Engineer Pass Trail, the route can be commenced at Silverton by taking the road to Animas Forks (Southwest #6) and then the North Fork Cutoff (Southwest #5) to connect with Engineer Pass Trail.

The turnoff from US 550 onto Engineer Pass Trail is well marked with a national forest access sign. This 4WD track gets straight down to business. In fact, the next five miles are the hardest of the entire trip. Sections of the road are steep and rough. It is also narrow with sheer drop-offs. Although it may appear threatening at first, it is readily passable for 4WD vehicles if taken slowly and carefully.

A tip for those who are nervous about driving shelf roads and encountering oncoming vehicles: Leave early. This road is popular, and oncoming 4WD vehicles will be encountered frequently later in the day, as those traveling from Lake City are descending. Pull-offs are reasonably frequent.

At the 1.6-mile point, you pass the Mickey Breene Mine, which was discovered in 1890. The mine yielded high-grade ore and produced copper and silver.

About two and one-half miles from US 550, the road intersects with the Poughkeepsie 4WD road. This road is difficult and should be taken only by those willing to risk vehicle damage.

From the Mineral Point turnoff, the terrain starts to clear, with numerous open, although boggy meadows. The climb continues to Engineer Pass at 12,750 feet.

From the summit, the road descends through the southern edge of American Flats and past the site of Engineer City.

From this point, the road follows the path of Henson Creek all the way to Lake City.

About two miles after the summit, there is a scenic old cabin beside the creek at Palmetto Gulch; shortly after that, a bridge crosses the creek at what was the site of the Palmetto Gulch Mill. From this point, the road is passable by passenger vehicles.

The road passes close by Rose's Cabin, which was an important way station on the stage route. The remains of the buildings can still be seen.

Less than a mile further is the Empire

Chief Mill that was worked from January to March 1929, when an avalanche killed four men and destroyed most of the buildings.

A few miles on, a sign marks a short walking trail down to beautiful Whitmore Falls. Though short, the hike back up is strenuous.

The original Capitol City, with its grand aspirations to be the state capital, is now reduced to the remains of the post office. However, the town site is on private land, and new homes continue to be built there.

The route continues to Henson and then through Henson Creek Canyon to Lake City.

Bulldozers plow portions of Engineer Pass, which is usually opened around mid-June. When the road crews get through, they leave in their wake a narrow channel through the snow, with walls of snow up to twenty feet high on either side.

Current Road Condition Information

San Juan National Forest
701 Camino del Rio
Durango, CO 81301
(970) 247-4874

Lake City Chamber of Commerce
3rd and Silver Streets
Lake City, CO 81235
(970) 944-2527

Silverton Chamber of Commerce
414 Greene Street
Silverton, CO 81433
(970) 387-5654

Map References

USFS   Uncompahgre NF or Gunnison NF
USGS   Hinsdale County #1
          Ouray County #2
          San Juan County
Trails Illustrated, #141
The Roads of Colorado, p. 115
Colorado Atlas & Gazetteer, pp. 67, 77

Route Directions

▼ 0.0   In front of Beaumont Hotel at 5th and Main in Ouray, zero trip meter and proceed south out of town, remaining on US 550.

3.7 ▲   End in front of Beaumont Hotel at 5th and Main in Ouray.
GPS: N 38°01.30' W 107°40.29'

▼ 3.7   TL   National Forest access sign on right. Engineer Mountain and Alpine Loop signs are at the dirt track entrance. Zero trip meter.

0.0 ▲   Proceed on US 550 toward Ouray. Paved road.
GPS: N 37°59.26' W 107°39.01'

▼ 0.0   Proceed along jeep trail.

7.0 ▲   TR   Intersection with US 550. Zero trip meter.

▼ 1.6   SO   Mickey Breene Mine ruins on left.

5.4 ▲   SO   Mickey Breene Mine ruins on right.

▼ 1.7   SO   Private road on left.

5.3 ▲   SO   Private road on right.

▼ 2.0   SO   Diamond Creek crossing. Track on right to backcountry campsites.

5.0 ▲   SO   Track on left to backcountry campsites. Diamond Creek crossing.

▼ 2.4   TL   Poughkeepsie Gulch 4WD trail to the right.

4.6 ▲   BR   Intersection with Poughkeepsie Gulch 4WD trail on the left.
GPS: N 37°58.01' W 107°37.60'

▼ 3.4   SO   Track on left.

3.6 ▲   SO   Track on right.

▼ 3.7   SO   Track on right to backcountry campsites.

3.3 ▲   SO   Track on left to backcountry campsites.

▼ 4.2   SO   Miner's cabin on left. Tracks on left to Des Ouray Mine.

2.8 ▲   SO   Tracks on right to Des Ouray Mine. Cabin on right.

▼ 4.4   SO   Track on right. Stay on main road.

2.6 ▲   SO   Track on left. Stay on main road.

▼ 4.6   SO   Track on right to backcountry campsites.

2.4 ▲   SO   Track on left to backcountry campsites.

▼ 5.0   SO   Track on right to backcountry campsites.

2.0 ▲   SO   Track on left to backcountry campsites.

▼ 5.1   TL   Intersection: Signpost to Mineral Point. Follow sign to Engineer Mountain.

1.9 ▲   BR   Intersection.
GPS: N 37°57.72' W 107°35.71'

▼ 5.2   SO   View across the valley to San Juan Chief Mill.

1.8 ▲   SO   View across the valley to San Juan Chief Mill.

▼ 5.8   SO   Public restrooms on right.

1.2 ▲   SO   Public restrooms on left.

▼ 6.1   SO   Tracks on right lead to series of open mine portals.

0.9 ▲   SO   Tracks on left lead to series of open mine portals.

▼ 7.0   TL   Intersection with Southwest #5: North Fork Cutoff. Signs indicate Silverton and Animas Forks to the right; Lake City via Engineer Pass to the left. Zero trip meter.

0.0 ▲   Continue toward Ouray.
GPS: N 37°57.42' W 107°34.47'

▼ 0.0   Continue on main road toward Engineer Pass.

6.1 ▲   TR   Three-way intersection. Straight ahead is Southwest #5: North Fork Cutoff, which leads to Animas Forks and Silverton. Zero trip meter.

▼ 0.8   UT   Follow sign to Engineer Pass. An unmarked track is straight ahead.

5.3 ▲   UT   Unmarked track is straight ahead.

▼ 1.9   SO   Road on left to Oh! Point.

SW Trail #1: Engineer Pass Trail

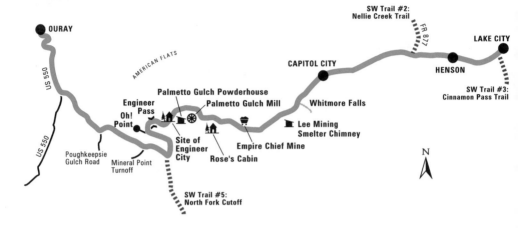

4.2 ▲ SO Road on right to Oh! Point.

▼ 2.3 BR Summit of Engineer Pass. Two walking track trailheads are at summit: Bear Creek and Ridge Stock Driveway. Follow sign to Lake City.

3.8 ▲ BL Summit of Engineer Pass. Two walking track trailheads are at summit: Bear Creek and Ridge Stock Driveway.

GPS: N 37°58.46' W 107°35.08'

▼ 2.5 SO Frank Hough Mine remains and American Flats.

3.6 ▲ SO Frank Hough Mine remains and American Flats.

▼ 2.8 SO Site of Engineer City.
3.3 ▲ SO Site of Engineer City.

▼ 3.2 SO Horsethief Trail walking track on left.
2.9 ▲ SO Horsethief Trail walking track on right.

▼ 3.4 SO Palmetto Gulch powderhouse and mine remains on right. Track on right to open mine shaft.

2.7 ▲ SO Track on left to open mine portal. Palmetto Gulch powderhouse and mine remains on left.

▼ 4.4 SO Palmetto Gulch cabin.
1.7 ▲ SO Palmetto Gulch cabin.

▼ 4.6 SO Thoreau's Cabin on left.

1.5 ▲ SO Thoreau's Cabin on right.

▼ 4.8 SO Bridge and Palmetto Gulch mill remains. 2WD vehicles sufficient from this point onward.

1.3 ▲ SO Palmetto Gulch mill remains and bridge. 4WD vehicles recommended beyond this point.

▼ 5.1 SO Track on right to backcountry campsites along Henson Creek. Track networks with next two entries.

1.0 ▲ SO Track on left to backcountry campsites along Henson Creek.

▼ 5.4 SO Track on right goes to same vicinity as previous. Also goes across creek to Hurricane Basin and past a mine.

0.7 ▲ SO Track on left to backcountry campsites along Henson Creek.

▼ 6.1 BL Road to Rose's Cabin site on right. Zero trip meter.

0.0 ▲ Continue along main road toward Engineer Pass.

GPS: N 37°58.58' W 107°32.20'

▼ 0.0 SO Continue along main road toward Lake City.

9.0 ▲ BR Road to Rose's Cabin site on left. Zero trip meter.

▼ 0.1 SO Public restrooms on right.

8.9 ▲	SO	Public restrooms on left.

▼ 0.8	SO	Empire Chief Mine and Mill on left.
8.2 ▲	SO	Empire Chief Mine and Mill on right.

▼ 1.2	SO	Waterfall on right.
7.8 ▲	SO	Waterfall on left.

▼ 2.4	SO	Smelter chimney on right from the Lee Mining and Smelter Company.
6.6 ▲	SO	Smelter chimney on left from the Lee Mining and Smelter Company.

▼ 3.4	SO	Whitmore Falls walking track on right.
5.6 ▲	SO	Whitmore Falls walking track on left.

▼ 4.5	SO	Corral on right.
4.5 ▲	SO	Corral on left.

▼ 5.0	SO	Capitol City town site. Private land and new homes.
4.0 ▲	SO	Capitol City town site.

GPS: N 38°00.35′ W 107°28.05′

▼ 5.1	BR	Bridge, then signpost on left indicating road to N. Henson Road via Matterhorn Creek and Uncompahgre Peak.
3.9 ▲	BL	Walking trails on right, then bridge.

▼ 7.1	SO	Bridge and track on right.
1.9 ▲	SO	Bridge and track on left.

▼ 8.6	SO	Open mine portal on left along road.
5.5 ▲	SO	Open mine portal on right along road.

▼ 8.9	SO	Public restrooms on left.
0.4 ▲	SO	Public restrooms on right.

▼ 9.0	SO	Track on left is Southwest #2: Nellie Creek Trail. Zero trip meter.
0.1 ▲	SO	Continue on main road toward Engineer Pass.

GPS: N 38°01.22′ W 107°23.97′

▼ 0.0		Continue on main road toward Lake City.
5.1 ▲	SO	Track on right is Southwest #2: Nellie Creek Trail. Zero trip meter.

▼ 1.3	SO	Town of Henson.

3.7 ▲	SO	Town of Henson.

▼ 1.7	SO	Open mine portal on left along road.
3.4 ▲	SO	Open mine portal on right along road.

▼ 2.5	SO	Alpine Gulch Trailhead on right.
2.6 ▲	SO	Alpine Gulch Trailhead on left.

▼ 4.0	SO	Ruins of old mill on left.
1.2 ▲	SO	Ruins of old mill on right.

▼ 5.1	TR	Stop sign in Lake City. At next intersection, TL onto Silver Street.
0.1 ▲	TR	Onto Second Street, then TL at next intersection.

▼ 5.2		End in front of the Lake City Visitor Information Center at 306 Silver Street.
0.0 ▲		In front of the Lake City Visitor Information Center at 306 Silver (main) Street, zero trip meter and proceed south.

GPS: N 38°01.76′ W 107°18.98′

Nellie Creek Trail

STARTING POINT Intersection of Southwest #1: Engineer Pass Trail and FR 877
FINISHING POINT Uncompahgre Peak Trailhead
TOTAL MILEAGE 4 miles (one-way)
UNPAVED MILEAGE 4 miles
DRIVING TIME 3/4 hour
ROUTE ELEVATION 9,400 to 11,500 feet
USUALLY OPEN Mid-June to early October
DIFFICULTY RATING 4
SCENIC RATING 8

Special Attractions

- Interesting side road from Engineer Pass Trail.
- Scenery ranging from waterfalls to spectacular Uncompahgre Peak.
- Access to Uncompahgre Trailhead and the numerous hiking trails of the Uncompahgre Wilderness.

An early section of the trail that travels beside Nellie Creek

History

From much of the higher section of this trail you view the towering Uncompahgre Peak. At 14,309 feet, it is the highest mountain in the San Juans and the sixth highest in Colorado. The Hayden Survey party made the first recorded ascent in 1874 and it was also climbed by Lt. William Marshall of the later Wheeler Survey. Prior to these times, the Ute used the peak as a lookout.

Hikers find the north face treacherous to climb, but access from the southwest and southeast is relatively easy. The mountain became notorious for its large population of grizzly bears, which was mentioned by both the survey parties. However, evidently not everyone was deterred by their presence because in the late 1800s, the peak became a popular excursion for parties of hikers from the nearby mining towns of Capitol City and Lake City.

No major mines were ever found on the mountain itself.

Description

The initial section of this road is a gentle climb through the forest following the course of Nellie Creek. This lower section of the creek and the nearby forest show the signs of many industrious beavers' labor. The trail is rough with occasional loose boulders, but generally they are embedded and it is not difficult to drive in a high-clearance vehicle. The biggest problem you are likely to have is passing vehicles you encounter traveling the other way, as some sections are too narrow to pass without one driver reversing to a suitable spot.

There are numerous aspen trees at the lower reaches that add color in the fall to the already very attractive scenery provided by the Nellie Creek, which flows beside the trail for much of the route, and a waterfall located at the 0.7-mile point.

After about three-quarters of a mile, there is a section of shelf road upon which you continue the climb. The road levels off after a little more than a mile and a half and you get a good view of Uncompahgre Peak. After you cross a shallow creek, the climb through the forest continues. The trail switchbacks up to another relatively level segment that can become quite boggy in wet weather conditions. The trail becomes rougher at this

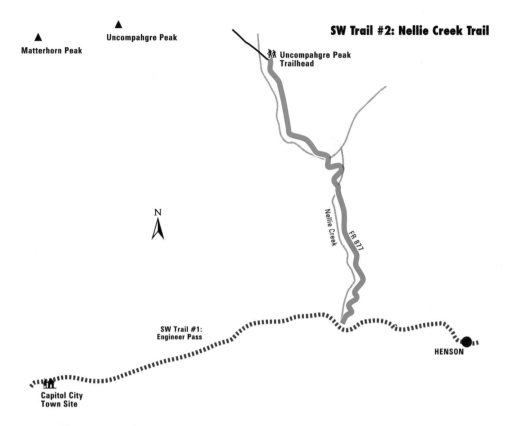

time and there are a number of shallow creek crossings. This section is the most difficult part of the trail but under dry conditions it only just warrants a rating of 4.

After about three miles, the trail levels off and enters an alpine meadow. A mile further, the trail ends at the parking area for the Uncompahgre Peak Trailhead.

Current Road Condition Information

Gunnison National Forest
Gunnison Ranger District
216 N. Colorado
Gunnison, CO 81230
(970) 641-0471

Lake City Chamber of Commerce
3rd and Silver Streets
Lake City, CO 81235
(970) 944-2527

Map References

USFS Gunnison NF or Uncompahgre NF
USGS Hinsdale #1

Trails Illustrated, #141
The Roads of Colorado, p. 115
Colorado Atlas & Gazetteer, p. 67

Route Directions

▼ 0.0   From Southwest #1: Engineer Pass Trail (5.1 miles from Lake City), zero trip meter and proceed along the 4WD track with sign to Nellie Creek Trailhead and Uncompahgre Peak Trail (FR 877).
GPS: N 38°01.22' W 107°23.97'

▼ 0.7   SO Waterfall in trees on left.
▼ 1.6   SO Beaver lodge on right.
▼ 1.7   SO Great view of rugged Uncompahgre Peak.
▼ 1.8   SO Cross through Nellie Creek.
GPS: N 38°02.58' W 107°24.23'

▼ 2.2   SO Ruins of two log buildings across creek.
▼ 2.3   UT Short track on right.

▼ 2.6	SO	Cross through creek.
▼ 3.4	SO	Cross through creek.
▼ 4.0		Public restrooms. Then end of track at trailhead and parking area.

GPS: N 38°03.74' W 107°25.32'

Cinnamon Pass Trail

STARTING POINT Lake City at intersection with Southwest #1: Engineer Pass Trail
FINISHING POINT Animas Forks
TOTAL MILEAGE 26.8 miles
UNPAVED MILEAGE 20.4 miles
DRIVING TIME 2 hours
ROUTE ELEVATION 8,932 to 12,620 feet
USUALLY OPEN Late May to late October
DIFFICULTY RATING 3
SCENIC RATING 9

Special Attractions

- Animas Forks ghost town.
- Part of the Alpine Loop, with many historic mining towns.
- Moderately easy 4WD trail opened by snowplow early in the season.
- Wonderful, varied scenery.

History

The Ute used this pass road before white exploration of the area. Then, in the early 1860s, Charles Baker used the pass on his journey into the San Juans when he reported finding gold, triggering a minor gold rush.

Burrows Park

In 1873, Albert Burrows further explored the area; and in the following year, the Hayden Survey party crossed the pass.

In the mid-1870s, Washington bureaucrats came to the conclusion that because the pass was not on the Continental Divide, the mail service should be able to cross it all year long; they awarded a contract on just that basis, despite the impossibility of the task.

In 1877, Enos Hotchkiss constructed the first wagon road over the pass. It was an important freight road for a period but was not maintained after the ore in the area declined.

The route starts at the still active town of Lake City. It was established following the discovery of the Golden Fleece Mine in 1874, originally named the Hotchkiss Mine, which became the best producer in the area although many other strikes followed.

In 1875, Lake City, named for nearby Lake San Cristobal, was registered and stagecoaches began making three trips a week to Saguache. That same year, Harry M. Woods published Lake City's first newspaper, the *Silver World*. The post office opened when the stagecoach service was extended to include a mail stage to Del Norte.

Lake City was one of the first towns in Colorado to have telephone service. In 1876, Western Union initiated telephone service and by 1881, service had been extended to Silverton, Ouray, Capitol City, Rose's Cabin, Mineral Point, and Animas Forks. Musicians utilized the telephone service to perform popular telephone concerts for listeners along the various lines!

At its high point, Lake City had around 2,500 residents. Since the town was platted at the junction of two toll roads—Saguache to Silverton and Antelope Springs to Lake City—hundreds of people passed through the community each week. Stagecoaches continued to stop in the city daily. The Denver & Rio Grande Railroad arrived in 1889. There were two trains daily in the 1890s, and ore shipments left regularly.

The wild red-light district on the west of

THE CANNIBALISM OF ALFERD PACKER

Alferd Packer was born in Pennsylvania. He served for a short time in the Union army during the Civil War and was discharged due to "disability." Packer, like many other men of his era, migrated westward with hopes of finding fabulous riches at the end of his arduous journey. He never made a fortune; he simply bummed around the mining camps, prospecting on occasion.

In November 1873, Packer led a party of twenty-one men from Provo, Utah, to prospect in the San Juan Mountains of Colorado. Two months later, the group reached Ute Chief Ouray's winter camp at the junction of the Uncompahgre and Gunnison Rivers, near Montrose. Chief Ouray was friendly to the men and tried to warn them of the severe blizzards that regularly bombarded the mountains in the wintertime. Ouray tried to persuade the party to stay with him and his people to wait out the season. After a few days, Packer and five men decided they would continue their journey in search of gold, departing on February 9. The other sixteen men remained with Chief Ouray.

Alferd Packer

According to Packer, for some unknown reason, his group left camp with rations of only seven days' food for one man. It did not take the six men long to go through such a small supply, so after nearly a week, Packer separated from the group and ventured off in search of food.

In April, Packer arrived alone at Los Piños Indian Agency on Cochetopa Creek, carrying with him money and possessions from the other men in his party. The authorities' suspicions were aroused, and they questioned Packer about the fate of his five companions.

Packer claimed his companions had deserted him. He told the authorities that when he returned to camp after his fruitless search for food, he found one man sitting near the fire roasting a piece of meat cut from the leg of another man. Another three corpses lay near the fire; the head of each one had been bashed by a hatchet. Packer claimed that when the man saw him, he stood with his hatchet in hand, and Packer shot him through the belly.

In time, Packer finally admitted to killing the men and eating their bodies. He escorted a search party to recover the remains, but he quit the search before locating the bodies.

Packer was arrested and jailed in Saguache but escaped before he could be tried. Nine years later, he was arrested in Wyoming, where he had been living under another name.

In April 1883, he stood trial in Lake City and was found guilty and sentenced to hang the following month. An angry mob wanted to lynch him immediately, so he was moved to Gunnison for safekeeping.

Packer won a retrial, and his sentence was reduced to forty years at the State Prison in Canon City for manslaughter. He had served almost fifteen years when Governor Thomas pardoned him in 1901. As part of the pardon agreement, Packer moved to Denver, where for a while he worked as a doorman at the *Denver Post's* offices.

In April 1907, Packer died and was buried in Littleton Cemetery. A memorial plaque marking the site of the murders overlooks Lake San Cristobal on Cannibal Plateau.

---

town was known as Hell's Acres. Gambling dens and dance halls were interspersed among the many brothels. Lake City had its rough side: many of its residents were killed in mine accidents, snowslides, and shoot-outs.

Lake City experienced a series of eco-nomic fluctuations. It suffered greatly after the silver crash of 1893 and went into a long decline, relieved only by subsequent gold and lead production.

After the turn of the century, Lake City was on the decline; but camping, fishing,

American Basin

and hunting helped revive it as a summer community. In 1933, the railroad tracks were sold for scrap. Lake City never became a ghost town, although its population dwindled and it is currently a sleepy little community. Many buildings were made of stone and still survive. The large stone schoolhouse was built in 1882. The courthouse where Alferd Packer was tried was built in 1877 and is still used.

From Lake City, the paved road extends past Lake San Cristobal, which was initially formed in about A.D. 1270 by the Slumgullion Slide, a huge mud and rock slide. A second major slide about 350 years ago completed the formation of Lake San Cristobal and created the second largest natural lake in Colorado.

The route passes the turnoff to the town site of Sherman, which was founded in 1877 and named for an early pioneer. The town grew slowly at first, then expanded quickly in the 1880s. Although several mines in the area yielded large amounts of gold, silver, copper, and lead, the principal

mine was the Black Wonder. Located on the north side of town, the Black Wonder produced primarily silver. Sherman's population and prosperity fluctuated with the fortunes of the Black Wonder Mine, which continued to produce into the turn of the century. Most of the mine's ore was transported to smelters in Lake City. Sherman peaked in the mid-1880s, when the summer population reached about three hundred.

Sherman was a convenient stagecoach stop since it was located halfway between Animas Forks and Lake City. To travel on the toll road between Sherman and Lake City cost $2.50 and between Sherman and Animas Forks cost $2.00 in either direction.

Around 1900, a 150-foot dam was constructed upstream of Sherman, but only a few days after the dam's completion, runoff from torrential rains flooded the mountainside, ripped the dam to pieces, and swept away much of the town of Sherman. The silver crash three years later ended Sherman's hopes for recovery, although the town was not completely deserted until the 1920s.

A cluster of mining camps sprouted up in the alpine meadow of Burrows Park between 1877 and 1880. The park was five miles long and a half-mile wide. The exact locations of the camps are disputed, but the general area is about ten miles southwest of Lake City, at the western end of the valley.

Burrows Park was the name of one of the camps, founded in 1877. About a mile south of Burrows Park, there was a community named Tellurium. This very small camp had only about a dozen people, who hoped to find tellurium there. The highly optimistic group built an expensive mill. Unfortunately, Tellurium never became prosperous, and it soon was deserted. Sterling was located a short distance beyond Tellurium, toward Animas Forks. Nearer the Continental Divide toward Cinnamon Pass, Whitecross was the largest of the settlements and served as the center of activity for the other camps. Whitecross's post office, established in 1880, was first called Burrows Park, after the region. Two years later it was renamed Whitecross.

Many men who lived in this area worked at the Tabasco Mine and Mill, which operated from 1901 to 1904 and was one of the first to use electric alternating current. Tabasco, the Louisiana hot sauce manufacturing company, owned both the mine and the mill. Ruins of the mine are scattered around the summit of Cinnamon Pass.

Description

Today Cinnamon Pass Trail is a seasonal, moderately easy 4WD road. It is part of the historic and majestic Alpine Loop. The other half of the loop is Engineer Pass 4WD Trail (Southwest #1). These two roads form the backbone of a network of roads throughout the region. Cinnamon Pass Trail is the easier of the two, but in the peak summer months both are extremely popular 4WD routes.

The scenery varies from the rugged alpine environment of year-round snow and barren talus slopes near the summit to the wildflower-covered valleys and rushing streams draining the melting snow. At either end of the route are wonderful, historic towns, one a ghost town, the other very much alive.

Initially, the gravel road is an easy, maintained road. After entering the Gunnison National Forest, the road is intersected by the road to Wager Gulch on the left. This road (Southwest #4) goes to the ghost town of Carson and continues over the Continental Divide.

Three miles further along County 30 is the intersection with County 35—a short side road leading to the site of Sherman. While the remains of the town are clearly visible, the forest has reclaimed the entire area.

After the Sherman turnoff, the road narrows into a shelf road overlooking the canyon. However, it remains comfortably wide even for full-sized 4WD vehicles, with a sufficient number of pull-offs available to facilitate passing.

A short distance further, the road enters Burrows Park Basin—the region of Whitecross, Burrows Park, Tellurium, and Sterling townships. The road passes the two remaining buildings of Burrows Park (and a new public toilet).

About three and one-half miles further, after passing the turnoff to the American Basin, which is renowned for its spring wildflowers, the road becomes more difficult as it ascends above timberline into alpine tundra vegetation and offers expansive views. From the summit of Cinnamon Pass, the road descends into the picturesque ghost town of Animas Forks, which has numerous buildings remaining.

Bulldozers clear the snow on Cinnamon Pass, usually opening it by Memorial Day.

Current Road Condition Information

San Juan National Forest
701 Camino del Rio
Durango, CO 81301
(970) 247-4874

Lake City Chamber of Commerce
3rd and Silver Streets
Lake City, CO 81235
(970) 944-2527

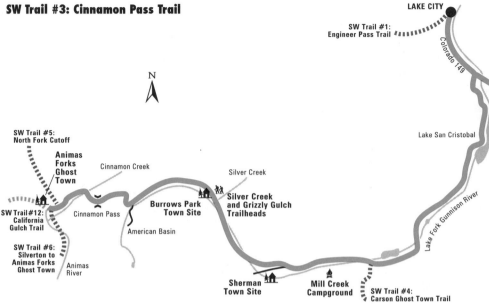

Silverton Chamber of Commerce
414 Greene Street
Silverton, CO 81433
(970) 387-5654

Map References

USFS   Uncompahgre NF or Gunnison NF
USGS Hinsdale County #1
        San Juan County
Trails Illustrated, #141
The Roads of Colorado, p. 115
Colorado Atlas & Gazetteer, pp. 67, 77

Route Directions

▼ 0.0   In front of the Lake City Information
        Center at 306 Silver (main) Street, zero
        trip meter and proceed south on Silver
        Street.
14.2 ▲   End at Lake City Information Center.
        GPS: N 38°01.76′ W 107°18.98′

▼ 0.1   TL Onto 2nd Street.
14.0 ▲   TR Onto Silver (main) Street.

▼ 0.2   TR Onto Gunnison Avenue (Colorado 149)
            toward Cinnamon Pass.
14.0 ▲   TL Onto 2nd Street.

▼ 2.4   TR Follow Alpine Loop Drive sign.
11.8 ▲ TL Onto Colorado 149.

▼ 6.4   BR Before bridge. Follow Alpine Loop sign
            onto unpaved road.
7.8 ▲   BL Bridge on right. Turn onto paved road.

▼ 9.1   SO USFS Williams Creek Campground on
            right.
5.1 ▲   SO USFS Williams Creek Campground on
            left.

▼ 11.3 SO Southwest #4: Carson Ghost Town
            Trail on left.
2.9 ▲   SO Southwest #4: Carson Ghost Town
            Trail on right.
            GPS: N 37°54.39′ W 107°21.60′

▼ 11.5 SO Cross over bridge.
2.7 ▲   SO Cross over bridge.

▼ 12.5 SO Public toilets on left.
1.7 ▲   SO Public toilets on right.

▼ 13.1 SO Mill Creek BLM campground on left.
1.1 ▲   SO Mill Creek BLM campground on right.

▼ 14.2 BR Intersection with County 35 on left to

Sherman town site. Follow sign to Cinnamon Pass and Silverton. Zero trip meter.

0.0 ▲ Continue on main road toward Lake City.
GPS: N 37°54.21′ W 107°24.68′

▼ 0.0 Continue on main road toward Cinnamon Pass.
7.5 ▲ SO Intersection with County 35 to Sherman town site on right. Zero trip meter.

▼ 0.5 SO Cross bridge.
7.0 ▲ SO Cross bridge.

▼ 3.9 SO Cross over Silver Creek.
3.7 ▲ SO Cross over Silver Creek.

▼ 4.0 SO Burrows Park town site. Grizzly Gulch (left) and Silver Creek (right) trailheads. Public toilets.
3.5 ▲ SO Burrows Park town site. Grizzly Gulch (right) and Silver Creek (left) trailheads. Public toilets.
GPS: N 37°56.24′ W 107°27.63′

▼ 5.5 SO Mine on right.
2.0 ▲ SO Mine on left.

▼ 6.3 SO Cattle guard.
1.3 ▲ SO Cattle guard.

▼ 6.4 SO Creek crossing.
1.1 ▲ SO Creek crossing.

▼ 7.1 SO Track on left leads to mines.
0.4 ▲ SO Track on right leads to mines.

▼ 7.4 SO Creek cascade on right flows underneath road.
0.2 ▲ SO Creek cascade on left flows underneath road.

▼ 7.6 BR Intersection. Posted sign reads "4WD recommended past this point." American Basin on left. Zero trip meter.
0.0 ▲ Continue on main road toward Lake City.
GPS: N 37°55.87′ W 107°30.80′

▼ 0.0 Continue on main road toward Cinnamon Pass.
2.2 ▲ BL Intersection. American Basin on right. Zero trip meter.

▼ 0.4 SO Cross over creek.
1.8 ▲ SO Cross over creek.

▼ 0.5 SO Deserted cabin on right and then Tabasco Mill ruins.
1.6 ▲ SO Tabasco Mill ruins and then deserted cabin on left.

▼ 2.2 SO Summit of Cinnamon Pass. Zero trip meter.
0.0 ▲ Continue on main road toward Lake City.
GPS: N 37°56.03′ W 107°32.25′

▼ 0.0 Continue on main road toward Animas Forks.
2.8 ▲ SO Summit of Cinnamon Pass. Zero trip meter.

▼ 0.1 BL Track on right.
2.7 ▲ BR Track on left.

▼ 0.7 SO Cross over Cinnamon Creek.
2.1 ▲ SO Cross over Cinnamon Creek.

▼ 2.1 UT Track straight ahead is Southwest #5: North Fork Cutoff. Continue on main road.
0.7 ▲ UT Follow switchback toward Cinnamon Pass. Straight ahead is Southwest #5: North Fork Cutoff.

▼ 2.5 UT Intersection. Go toward Animas Forks. Silverton is straight ahead.
0.3 ▲ UT Intersection. Follow switchback toward Cinnamon Pass. Silverton is straight ahead.
GPS: N 37°55.78′ W 107°33.90′

▼ 2.8 Cross bridge into Animas Forks and end at intersection. Southwest #6 to Silverton is to the left; Southwest #12: California Gulch Trail is to the right.

Carson ghost town, nestled in Wager Gulch

SOUTHWEST REGION TRAIL #4

Carson Ghost Town Trail

STARTING POINT Intersection of Southwest #3: Cinnamon Pass Trail and FR 568
FINISHING POINT Carson Ghost Town
TOTAL MILEAGE 3.7 miles (one-way)
UNPAVED MILEAGE 3.7 miles
DRIVING TIME 30 minutes
ROUTE ELEVATION 9,400 to 12,350 feet
USUALLY OPEN Mid-June to late September
DIFFICULTY RATING 4
SCENIC RATING 9

Special Attractions
■ Well-preserved ghost town of Carson.
■ Views from the Continental Divide.

History
Following the discovery of silver at Carson in 1881, a wagon road was built to service the mines, leading from the Gunnison River to Lake City. Carson was very close to the Continental Divide and was one of the most remote mining camps in Colorado. The sil-

Stalls in the Carson ghost town stables

ver crash of 1893 led to its demise, and no buildings remain standing.

In 1896, prospectors discovered gold in the area, and a new town was built at a lower elevation than the original. It is this second town of Carson that remains today as a ghost town. It was abandoned in 1903; the road that serviced it also fell into disuse.

Description
This short side trip from Cinnamon Pass Trail offers a very well-preserved ghost town, spectacular panoramic views from the crest of the Continental Divide, and more often than not, a section of very slippery mud to contend with.

The route commences from Southwest #3: Cinnamon Pass Trail, 15.4 miles from Animas Forks and 11.3 miles from Lake City. A sign that reads "Wager Gulch/ Carson" marks the turnoff.

The road is initially fairly steep but reasonably wide and has an adequate number of pull-offs. Occasional rocks in the road and eroded surfaces can require care in selecting the right line, but the road should not be too rough for a normal 4WD vehicle.

The most difficult problem can be mud. The first two miles of this trail are usually spotted with muddy sections. The surface is firm, but it can be very slippery and wheel-rutted and because the road is sheltered by the forest, muddy conditions are very slow to dry out.

Getting adequate traction depends on the weight of your vehicle, the state of the road on the day you attempt it, and, most importantly, the tires you are using. Exercise care in order to avoid oncoming vehicles that can have difficulty steering or stopping on the downhill slope.

Once you pass the mud, this road is straightforward. A visit to Carson and the views from the Continental Divide make it well worthwhile.

The Continental Divide is just over a mile past the creek crossing at Carson. From the Continental Divide, the route deteriorates into walking trails so you'll need to retrace your tracks and return to Cinnamon Pass Trail.

Current Road Condition Information

Gunnison National Forest
Gunnison Ranger District
216 N. Colorado
Gunnison, CO 81230
(970) 641-0471

Map References

USFS Uncompahgre NF or Gunnison NF
USGS Hinsdale County #1
Trails Illustrated, #141
The Roads of Colorado, pp. 115, 131
Colorado Atlas & Gazetteer, p. 77

Route Directions

▼ 0.0 From intersection of Southwest #3: Cinnamon Pass Trail and FR 568, zero trip meter and proceed toward Carson on FR 568. This intersection is 11.3 miles from Lake City.
    GPS: N 37°54.39′ W 107°21.60′

▼ 0.1 BL Series of private driveways.
▼ 0.7 SO Creek crossing.
▼ 1.7 BR Fork in road. Continue uphill.
▼ 2.2 SO Creek crossing.
▼ 2.8 SO Cabin ruins on left.
▼ 3.5 BL Fork in road. Turn toward Carson ghost

SW Trail #4: Carson Ghost Town Trail

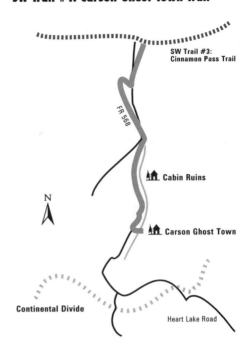

town. Straight ahead will lead across the Continental Divide and to the site of Old Carson.

▼ 3.6 SO Cross through creek.
▼ 3.7 BL Carson town site with many well-preserved structures.
    GPS: N 37°52.13′ W 107°21.72′

North Fork Cutoff

STARTING POINT Intersection with Southwest #3: Cinnamon Pass Trail
FINISHING POINT Intersection with Southwest #1: Engineer Pass Trail
TOTAL MILEAGE 2 miles
UNPAVED MILEAGE 2 miles
DRIVING TIME 20 minutes
ROUTE ELEVATION 11,489 to 12,169 feet
USUALLY OPEN Late May to late October
DIFFICULTY RATING 3
SCENIC RATING 4

Denver Lake and open mine portals along the North Fork Cutoff

Description

This route is straightforward and is included in this book to allow more flexibility in undertaking the Alpine Loop, which primarily consists of Southwest #1: Engineer Pass Trail and Southwest #3: Cinnamon Pass Trail. By linking these two roads, the Alpine Loop can be started or finished from any of three towns: Lake City, Ouray, or Silverton.

The North Fork Cutoff usually opens before the summit of Engineer Pass is cleared, allowing access to the western end of Engineer Pass Trail, which can be used as a route between Ouray and Animas Forks.

Although the route includes sections of shelf road, it is not very narrow and has a reasonable number of pull-offs. However, it is sufficiently rough to require a high-clearance vehicle.

Current Road Condition Information

San Juan National Forest
701 Camino del Rio
Durango, CO 81301
(970) 247-4874

Map References

USFS Uncompahgre NF or Gunnison NF
USGS San Juan County
Trails Illustrated, #141
The Roads of Colorado, p. 115
Colorado Atlas & Gazetteer, p. 77

Route Directions

▼ 0.0   At the intersection of Southwest #3: Cinnamon Pass Trail and North Fork Cutoff, 0.7 miles from Animas Forks, zero trip meter and proceed north.

2.0 ▲   End at intersection with Cinnamon Pass Trail. Bear left to Lake City. Bear right to Animas Forks.

GPS: N 37°56.02' W 107°34.10'

▼ 0.3   SO Mine on left.
1.7 ▲   SO Mine on right.

▼ 0.4   SO Tram cables overhead.
1.6 ▲   SO Tram cables overhead.

▼ 0.6   SO Track on right.
1.4 ▲   SO Track on left.

▼ 0.9   SO Open mine portal in mountainside on the left.
1.1 ▲   SO Open mine portal in mountainside on the right.

▼ 1.0   SO Cross over creek.
1.0 ▲   SO Cross over creek.

▼ 1.2   SO Cross over creek.
0.8 ▲   SO Cross over creek.

▼ 1.4   BR Open mine portal on left. Track on left

leads to mines along Burrows Creek and dead-ends in approximately 2 miles. Follow sign to Engineer Pass and Alpine Loop.

0.6 ▲ BL Track on right leads to mines along Burrows Creek and dead-ends. Open mine portal on right.
GPS: N 37°56.91' W 107°34.53'

▼ 1.6 SO Track on left to Denver Lake, cabin, and mine. Cross over creek. Track on right.

0.4 ▲ SO Track on left. Cross over creek. Track on right to Denver Lake, cabin, and mine.

▼ 1.7 SO Mine ruins on right.
0.3 ▲ SO Mine ruins on left.

▼ 2.0   End at intersection with Southwest #1: Engineer Pass Trail. Left goes to Ouray. Right goes to Engineer Pass and Lake City.

0.0 ▲   At the intersection of Southwest #1: Engineer Pass Trail and North Fork Cutoff, zero trip meter and proceed south along North Fork Cutoff toward Animas Forks.
GPS: N 37°57.41' W 107°34.48'

Silverton to Animas Forks Ghost Town

STARTING POINT Silverton
FINISHING POINT Animas Forks
TOTAL MILEAGE 12.1 miles
UNPAVED MILEAGE 10.0 miles
DRIVING TIME 45 minutes
ROUTE ELEVATION 9,400 to 11,370 feet
USUALLY OPEN Mid-May to late October
DIFFICULTY RATING 1
SCENIC RATING 8

Special Attractions

■ Animas Forks, one of Colorado's best ghost towns.

SW Trail #5: North Fork Cutoff

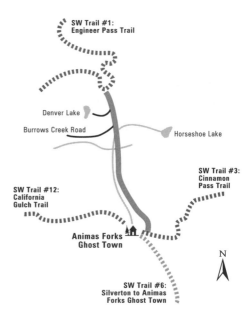

SW Trail #1: Engineer Pass Trail

Denver Lake

Burrows Creek Road

Horseshoe Lake

SW Trail #3: Cinnamon Pass Trail

SW Trail #12: California Gulch Trail

Animas Forks Ghost Town

N

SW Trail #6: Silverton to Animas Forks Ghost Town

■ The extremely historic road following the old railway grade, with innumerable points of historic interest.

History

This route commences at Silverton, a well-preserved, historic mining town that was founded in 1873. It is the terminus for the famed Durango and Silverton Narrow Gauge Railroad, which is extremely popular with tourists in the summer months.

From Silverton, the route follows the Animas River as it passes numerous mines that line the sides of the area known as Bakers Park, which extends all the way to Eureka. The park was named after Charles Baker, one of the first explorers in the area, who triggered a minor gold rush into territory still defended by the Ute in the early 1860s.

At the six-mile point is the town site of Middleton, a small mining camp in the late 1800s, of which nothing remains. At the 7.7-mile point is the town site of Eureka. At the southern end of the town site is a turnoff on the right, which in days gone bye was Saguache Street and led into the center of

ANIMAS FORKS

Animas Forks, originally called La Plata City, experienced its first silver strike in 1875. As an enticement to live near timberline and brave the harsh winters, the government offered settlers free lots and aid for building homes.

Within a year, settlers had erected thirty cabins, a post office, a saloon, a general store, a hotel, and two mills; the town soon boasted a population of two hundred. All the buildings were well constructed, with finished lumber and shingled roofs. The jailhouse, a rough, box-like structure made of two-by-six lumber and consisting of two cells and a jailer's office in front, was a rare exception to the general building standards.

In 1877, Otto Mears constructed a wagon road to Eureka and through to Silverton. This resulted in his network of toll roads connecting Lake City, Ouray, and Silverton. Animas

Forks became the central junction for these and other roads that connected the area's many mining camps. The other main contributor to the town's economy was its mill, which treated ore from Red Cloud Mine in Mineral Point.

Snow presented a huge problem for Animas Forks. Although the town was considered a year-round mining community, the population dropped in the wintertime. In 1884, the population reached four hundred in the summer but dropped to a dozen men, three women, and

A view of Animas Forks in 1875

twenty dogs in the winter. A winter storm that same year lasted for twenty-three days.

During the 1880s, telephone lines were installed, running from Lake City and passing over the 12,500-foot Continental Divide near Engineer Pass. Stagecoaches ran daily from Lake City to Silverton via Engineer Pass.

Mrs. Eckard, the first woman in Animas Forks, ran an extremely popular boardinghouse. Eckard won the favor of the local miners by extending them credit. When one freeloader slipped out of town without settling his account for three months' lodging, a vigilante committee set out after him. They caught him in Silverton and threatened to lynch him. He paid up, and no further bad debts were reported!

At its peak, Animas Forks was home to about 1,500 residents. Located at an elevation of 11,584 feet, it once boasted that it was the largest city in the world at this altitude.

Although its prosperity began to wane by the 1890s and the town was nearly deserted by 1901, Animas Forks experienced a resurgence of activity between 1904 and 1916. Otto Mears extended the railroad in 1904 and planned an elaborate system of seven snowsheds to permit the line to operate from Lake City to Silverton. Snowdrifts in the area were sometimes over twenty-five feet high. When the first big snowslide of the season destroyed the first of Mears's sheds, his idea was abandoned. The remains of this shed are clearly visible along Southwest #6: Silverton to Animas Forks Ghost Town.

The Gold Prince Mill, constructed in 1904, operated until 1910 and was moved to Eureka in 1917. Animas Forks rapidly declined once more.

In 1942, the railroad tracks were removed and scrapped. The railroad bed became a road again after the tracks were removed.

Today, Animas Forks is a fascinating ghost town, consisting of about a dozen houses. The Columbus Mill still stands, as do several other structures, including an elaborate house with a bay window. The foundations of the Gold Prince Mill remain at the southern end of town.

A view of Eureka and the Sunnyside Mill

town. The square building is the restored water tank; the room below was used as the town jail. The foundations of several other buildings are evident.

The massive foundations that rise up the mountainside on the other side of the Animas River are the remains of the Sunnyside Mill. The Sunnyside Mine, located in Eureka Gulch behind the mill, was discovered in 1873. By 1910 it consisted of ten miles of tunnel and employed three hundred miners. The first wooden mill opened in 1899 to the left of the existing foundations, which belong to the second Sunnyside Mill (which started production in 1918). The second mill incorporated much of the dismantled Gold Prince Mill, relocated from Animas Forks.

About half a mile from Eureka, the ruins of a boardinghouse and a bridge across the Animas River can be seen on the right. The boardinghouse was built in 1907 to house the workers from the Tom Moore Mine.

The road at this point follows the old

Silverton Northern Railroad line built by Otto Mears in 1903–1904. Four hundred men worked on this stage of the railroad line; it had an average grade of 7 percent, which resulted in the train having an average speed of only four miles per hour. Going up, the train could only pull a coal car and one empty car, and on the downhill, it was

The Casey Jones

limited to a maximum of three ore cars.

The other natural obstacle that challenged the railroad was snow. On the left of the road can be seen the remnants of one of the snowsheds built by Otto Mears to protect the railroad from the snowslides prevalent in the area. Despite Mears's best endeavors, nature proved too strong an adversary, and the snowsheds were destroyed in the first winter. High operating costs and declining mineral production led to the closure of the railroad in 1916.

Across the river from the snowshed can be seen the remnants of the last toll road built by Otto Mears in the mid-1880s—the only one he lost money on.

As you cross the Animas River on the entry into Animas Forks ghost town, the foundations on the right are the remains of the Gold Prince Mill, the largest concentrating mill in Colorado when it was built in 1904. On the left is the location of the railroad turntable used to turn around the steam engine of the Silverton Northern Railroad for the return to Silverton.

Further into Animas Forks, a number of buildings remain to the left of the road. The most famous of these is the two-story Walsh House, with the front bay window. This was home of William Duncan, built in 1879. It has been speculated that Thomas Walsh's daughter stayed there when writing her father's biography and also that Walsh rented a room there in his younger (and poorer) days. It is extremely unlikely that either story is true. The buildings across the Animas River as you leave town are the Columbus Mine and Mill, built in about 1880. This mill ceased operations in 1948.

Description

The entire route is an easy, well-maintained, gravel road suitable for passenger vehicles under good weather conditions.

Current Road Condition Information

San Juan National Forest
701 Camino del Rio
Durango, CO 81301
(970) 247-4874

Silverton Chamber of Commerce
414 Greene Street
Silverton, CO 81433
(970) 387-5654

Map References

USFS Uncompahgre NF or San Juan NF
USGS San Juan County
Trails Illustrated, #141
The Roads of Colorado, pp. 115, 131
Colorado Atlas & Gazetteer, p. 77

Route Directions

▼ 0.0		From the Silverton City Hall at Greene (main) Street and 14th Street, zero trip meter and proceed northeast out of town.
7.8 ▲		End in front of the Silverton City Hall at Greene and 14th Streets.
		GPS: N 37°48.79' W 107°39.72'
▼ 0.2	BR	Road forks. Bear right onto Colorado 110. Remain on paved road.
7.6 ▲	BL	Road forks. Bear left and remain on paved road.
▼ 0.4	SO	Campground on the right.
7.4 ▲	SO	Campground on the left.
▼ 0.5	SO	Lackawanna Mill on right across the river. Hillside Cemetery on left.
7.3 ▲	SO	Hillside Cemetery on right. Lackawanna Mill on left across the river.
▼ 0.7	BR	Road fork entering on left.
7.0 ▲	BL	Road fork entering on right.
▼ 1.6	SO	Aspen Mine ruins on right across the river.
6.2 ▲	SO	Aspen Mine ruins on left across the river.
▼ 1.7	SO	On the right side of the road, in the distance about 3 miles east, the tramhouse and boardinghouse of the Old Hundred Mine are evident about three-quarters of the way up Galena Mountain.

6.1 ▲ SO The tramhouse and boardinghouse of the Old Hundred Mine are evident on the left, in the distance about 3 miles southeast, three-quarters of the way up Galena Mountain.

▼ 2.0 SO Silver Lake Mill on right.
5.8 ▲ SO Silver Lake Mill on left.

▼ 2.1 SO Southwest #7: Arrastra Gulch Trail and Southwest #8: Silverton Northern Railroad Grade on right.
5.7 ▲ SO Southwest #7: Arrastra Gulch Trail and Southwest #8: Silverton Northern Railroad Grade on left.

▼ 2.2 SO Mayflower Mill and tram on left.
5.6 ▲ SO Mayflower Mill and tram on right.

▼ 3.8 SO Little Nation Mine on right, halfway up the mountainside.
4.0 ▲ SO Little Nation Mine on left, halfway up the mountainside.

▼ 4.0 SO Bridge across the Animas River.
3.8 ▲ SO Bridge across the Animas River.

▼ 4.2 SO Bridge across Cunningham Creek, then turnoff for Southwest #26: Cunningham Gulch and Stony Pass Trail on the right. Town site of Howardsville. Little Nations Mill.
3.6 ▲ SO Little Nations Mill. Town site of Howardsville. Turnoff for Southwest #26: Cunningham Gulch and Stony Pass Trail on the left. Bridge across Cunningham Creek.
GPS: N 37°50.06′ W 107°35.68′

▼ 6.0 SO Southwest #9: Maggie Gulch Trail on right. Town site of Middleton.
1.8 ▲ SO Town site of Middleton. Southwest #9: Maggie Gulch Trail on left.

▼ 6.6 SO Cross over creek. Southwest #10: Minnie Gulch Trail on right.
1.2 ▲SO Southwest #10: Minnie Gulch Trail on left. Cross over creek.

▼ 6.7 SO Track to campsites on right.

SW Trail #6: Silverton to Animas Forks Ghost Town

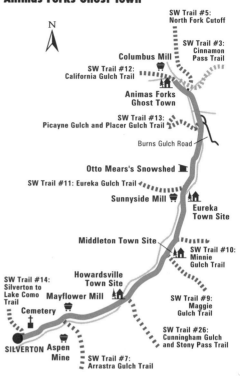

N

SW Trail #5: North Fork Cutoff

SW Trail #3: Cinnamon Pass Trail

Columbus Mill

SW Trail #12: California Gulch Trail

Animas Forks Ghost Town

SW Trail #13: Picayne Gulch and Placer Gulch Trail

Burns Gulch Road

Otto Mears's Snowshed

SW Trail #11: Eureka Gulch Trail

Sunnyside Mill

Eureka Town Site

Middleton Town Site

SW Trail #10: Minnie Gulch Trail

Howardsville Town Site

SW Trail #14: Silverton to Lake Como Trail

Mayflower Mill

SW Trail #9: Maggie Gulch Trail

Cemetery

SW Trail #26: Cunningham Gulch and Stony Pass Trail

SILVERTON Aspen Mine

SW Trail #7: Arrastra Gulch Trail

1.1 ▲ SO Track to campsites on left.

7.7 BL Entry to Eureka town site on right. Campsites.
0.1 ▲ BR Entry to Eureka town site on left. Campsites.

▼ 7.8 SO Bridge over Animas River. Zero trip meter.
0.0 ▲ Continue along main road.
GPS: N 37°52.76′ W 107°33.92′

▼ 0.0 Continue along main road.
4.3 ▲ SO Bridge over Animas River. Zero trip meter.

▼ 0.1 BR Sunnyside Mill on left.
4.2 ▲ BL Sunnyside Mill on right.

▼ 0.3 SO Southwest #11: Eureka Gulch Trail on left.
4.0 ▲ SO Southwest #11: Eureka Gulch Trail on right.

▼ 0.5	SO	Historic boardinghouse for mine workers on right.
3.7 ▲	SO	Historic boardinghouse for mine workers on left.

▼ 1.0	SO	Log remains of a snowshed built by Otto Mears on left.
3.3 ▲	SO	Log remains of a snowshed built by Otto Mears on right.

▼ 1.8	SO	Silver Wing Mine on right.
2.5 ▲	SO	Silver Wing Mine on left.

▼ 2.7	SO	Remains of dam used to feed the Silver Wing Mine.
1.6 ▲	SO	Remains of dam used to feed the Silver Wing Mine.

▼ 2.8	SO	Southwest #13: Picayne Gulch and Placer Gulch Trail on left. Track on right crosses Animas River and joins the road to Burns Gulch.
1.5 ▲	SO	Southwest #13: Picayne Gulch and Placer Gulch Trail on right. Track on left crosses Animas River and joins the road to Burns Gulch.

▼ 2.9	SO	Track on left. Cross over Animas River. Turnoff to Burns Gulch on right.
1.4 ▲	SO	Turnoff to Burns Gulch on left. Cross over Animas River. Track on right.

▼ 3.5	SO	Cross over Cinnamon Creek
0.8 ▲	SO	Cross over Cinnamon Creek

▼ 3.6	BL	Proceed toward Animas Forks. Cutoff to Cinnamon Pass Trail on right. Public restrooms on left.
0.7 ▲	BR	Public restrooms on right. Cutoff to Cinnamon Pass Trail on left. Proceed on main road toward Silverton.

▼ 3.9	SO	Cross over Animas River. Gold Prince Mill ruins on right.
0.4 ▲	SO	Gold Prince Mill ruins on left. Cross over Animas River.

▼ 4.1	SO	Public restrooms on right. Animas Forks jailhouse site behind the restrooms.
0.2 ▲	SO	Animas Forks jailhouse site behind the public restrooms on left.

▼ 4.3		Animas Forks ghost town. Bridge across Animas River is on the right, leading to Southwest #3: Cinnamon Pass and Southwest #1: Engineer Pass. The Columbus Mill is straight ahead.
0.0 ▲		At the bridge over the Animas Forks River at the north end of Animas Forks, zero trip meter and proceed south toward Silverton.

GPS: N 37°55.89′ W 107°34.22′

SOUTHWEST REGION TRAIL #7

Arrastra Gulch Trail

STARTING POINT Intersection with Southwest #6: Silverton to Animas Forks Ghost Town road

FINISHING POINT Gold Lake in Little Giant Basin

TOTAL MILEAGE 5.3 miles

UNPAVED MILEAGE 5.3 miles

DRIVING TIME 1 hour (one-way)

ROUTE ELEVATION 9,850 to 12,200 feet

USUALLY OPEN Mid-June to early October

DIFFICULTY RATING 5

SCENIC RATING 10

Special Attractions

■ Picturesque Gold Lake.
■ Black Prince mining camp.
■ Numerous other old mining remains.

History

The historic interest of this 4WD trail centers on the numerous mines that were located in the area. Many of the mining operations built mills to process their ore and tramways to transport the ore from the mines to the mills.

The first historic site along the route is the Whale Mill, which was an early, water-powered mill erected in about 1888 and eventually incorporated into the Silver Lake Mill operation.

Gold Lake

The Mayflower Mine was discovered in the late 1880s. Following construction of the Mayflower Mill in 1929, ore from the mine was carried nearly two miles by a steel tramway down to the mill for processing.

The Contention tramway carried ore one and one-quarter miles from the Big Giant and Black Prince mines to Contention Mill located on the north side of the Animas River, beside the railroad. Near the Black Prince Mine is a mining camp that still contains a number of long-deserted buildings. The mining company constructed them in 1915 to house its workers.

Near the end of the route is the Big Giant Mine, which was discovered in the 1870s but was only a marginal operation. After being bought by the Contention Mining Company, its tramway was used to carry ore to the Contention Mill for processing.

Description

This route is another side road of Colorado 110, the road between Silverton and Animas Forks (Southwest #6). It starts at the unmarked turnoff to Arrastra Gulch. Shortly after the start, you cross a bridge over the Animas River, and the shelf road that climbs toward Arrastra Gulch commences. As you progress along this road, there is a good view of the creek and valley below. The road is sound and reasonably wide.

At the 0.8-mile point, the road forks. The route directions follow the right-hand fork first and then return to explore the other fork. The right-hand section follows the gulch to end just below the Mayflower Mine, at which point the road gets much narrower and is washed out a short distance ahead.

The left-hand fork is the harder of the two roads. It goes to the Black Prince Mine and the buildings that have survived from the mining camp at the location. From there it climbs to the majestic surrounds of Gold Lake nestled in Little Giant Basin. This fork of the route starts by ascending a narrow shelf that has limited opportunity for passing. It is rough and rocky but not extremely

SW Trail #7: Arrastra Gulch Trail

and in the vicinity of Gold Lake. There are numerous aspens to provide autumn color in the lower section of the trail.

Current Road Condition Information
Silverton Chamber of Commerce
414 Greene Street
Silverton, CO 81433
(970) 387-5654

Map References
USFS   Uncompahgre NF or San Juan NF
USGS San Juan County
Trails Illustrated, #141
The Roads of Colorado, p. 131
Colorado Atlas & Gazetteer, p. 77

difficult because the surface is fairly sound. The rocks on the trail are not large enough to pose clearance problems for a 4WD vehicle, but some are sharp. From the Black Prince mining camp the road gets narrower with a very steep drop-off. The scenic location of Gold Lake makes the journey well worthwhile.

Most of this trail would rate a 3 for difficulty. The latter section, exploring the right-hand fork, rates a 4 until the Black Prince mining camp and a 5 for the last short section to Gold Lake. The trail is particularly scenic, especially along the upper reaches

Route Directions

▼ 0.0		From Southwest #6: Silverton to Animas Forks Ghost Town (County 110) opposite the Mayflower Mill, zero trip meter and proceed downhill on the Arrastra Gulch road towards the river. This intersection is 2.1 miles from Silverton City Hall. **GPS: N 37°49.62′ W 107°37.77′**
▼ 0.2	SO	Track on the left and right is Southwest #8: Silverton Northern Railroad Grade. Then cross Arrastra Creek.
▼ 0.3	SO	Cross under Mayflower Mill tram. Track on right goes to up Arrastra Gulch to the Silver Lake Mine.
▼ 0.5	SO	Ruins of dam in creek on right.
▼ 0.7	SO	Whale Mill ruins down at the creek on the other side. Level with the road, across the steam are the ruins of a wooden support for the Silver Lake Tram.
▼ 0.8	BL	Track straight ahead into meadow.
	BR	At the fork in the road. Zero trip meter. (You will return to this point to explore the left-hand fork.) **GPS: N 37.49.21′ W 107.37.23′**
▼ 0.0		Cross under tram line.
▼ 0.2	SO	Wooden tram structure on right.
▼ 0.3	SO	Track on left.

Big Giant Mill

▼ 0.6	SO	Track on left to Mayflower Mine and tram station.
▼ 0.7	SO	Cross under tram line. Tram towers on the right.
▼ 1.0	SO	Road deteriorates.
▼ 1.2	UT	Trail is washed out at head of gulch. Mayflower Mine on hill to the left. Turn around and return to the fork where you last reset the trip meter. **GPS: N 37°48.33' W 107°36.69'**

| ▼ 2.4 | TR | At intersection. Zero trip meter.
GPS: N 37°49.21' W 107°37.23' |

▼ 0.1	SO	Pass under tram cable.
▼ 0.3	SO	Both wooden and steel tram supports on right.
▼ 0.4	TL	Turn sharply onto the road to Little Giant Basin. **GPS: N 37°49.06' W 107°36.99'**

▼ 0.9	SO	Pass under tram cables for the Contention tram.
▼ 1.0	SO	Pass under tram cables.
▼ 1.3	SO	Pass under tram cables.
▼ 1.5	SO	Pass under tram cables.
▼ 2.1	BL	Black Prince mining camp. **GPS: N 37°48.35' W 107°36.29'**

▼ 2.4	SO	King Solomon Mine portal on left.
▼ 2.7	SO	Big Giant/Contention Mine and Mill on right.
▼ 2.9		End at beautiful Gold Lake. **GPS: N 37°48.39' W 107°35.96'**

SOUTHWEST REGION TRAIL #8

Silverton Northern Railroad Grade

STARTING POINT Intersection with Southwest #7: Arrastra Gulch Trail

FINISHING POINT Intersection with Southwest #6: Silverton to Animas Forks Ghost Town road, near Howardsville

TOTAL MILEAGE 2.6 miles

UNPAVED MILEAGE 2.6 miles

DRIVING TIME 1/2 hour

ROUTE ELEVATION 9,550 to 10,250 feet

USUALLY OPEN Mid-May to October

DIFFICULTY RATING 2

SCENIC RATING 8

Special Attractions

- Historic grade of the Silverton Northern Railroad.
- Remains of the Silver Lake Mill.
- Numerous other mining sites.

History

Otto Mears incorporated the Silverton Northern Railroad in November 1895 to connect Silverton to Animas Forks, which were fourteen miles apart.. His original plan was to then continue the tracks all the way to Lake City. The first stage to Howardsville and Eureka opened in June 1896. The second stage to Animas Forks opened in 1903, at an average grade of 7 percent. The line

The site of the Silver Lake Mill today

Silver Lake Mill, built in the 1890s

above Eureka was removed in 1920 and the lower section ceased operations in 1939; the tracks were removed in 1942. This route follows the old railroad grade from just below Arrastra Gulch to Howardsville.

The foundations of the Silver Lake Mill are a prominent feature along this route. The Silver Lake Mine had been discovered in about 1890 and had been greatly developed by the incorporation of further claims. The original claim was located at an altitude of 12,275 feet beside Silver Lake at the top of Arrastra Gulch. Two mills were built to process ore from this mine. The first was located at the mine. The second, more substantial mill was built in the late 1890s. This mill is still evident beside the Animas River and the Silverton Northern Railroad grade.

A tramway was constructed to carry ore over two and one-half miles from the mine to the new mill. The Silver Lake operation processed more than $7 million worth of ore before being bought by the Guggenheim empire in 1901 for $1.25 million. In 1906, the mill burned down. It was rebuilt but closed down in 1914. It burned down again in 1949 and what remained was sold for scrap.

The route also passes the site of the Wifley Mill. From 1913 to 1919, Otto Mears and Arthur Wifley leased the Silver Lake Mine and chose to process the ore, which they mainly recovered from the tailing dumps at the Wifley Mill, which was located on the north side of the Animas River at the bottom of Arrastra Gulch.

Description
The route starts a short distance along Southwest #7: Arrastra Gulch Trail. Initially, it heads southwest to the location of the Silver Lake Mill. This sections dead-ends after a short way at which point the route returns to the Arrastra Gulch road, crosses it and continues along the old railway grade all the way to Howardsville.

This trail, which is easy the entire length, is a very interesting short side route because of its mining and railroad history. It travels close beside the scenic Animas River.

Current Road Condition Information
Silverton Chamber of Commerce
414 Greene Street
Silverton, CO 81433
(970) 387-5654

Map References

USGS San Juan County (incomplete)
Trails Illustrated, #141 (incomplete)

Route Directions

▼ 0.0　From the 0.1 mile point along Southwest #7: Arrastra Gulch Trail, zero trip meter and turn right onto track that was once the Silverton Northern Railroad grade. This intersection is before Southwest #7 crosses the river.

1.0 ▲　End at intersection with Southwest #7: Arrastra Gulch Trail.

GPS: N 37°49.66′ W 107°37.63′

▼ 0.1　SO Site of the Wifley Mill on hillside to the right.

0.5 ▲　UT Fork in the road. Left crosses through creek. Right is closed. Turn around and retrace tracks.

▼ 0.2　SO Silver Lake Mill ruins across the Animas River on left.

0.2 ▲　SO Silver Lake Mill ruins across the Animas River on left.

▼ 0.5　UT Fork in the road. Left crosses through creek. Right closed. Turn around and retrace tracks.

0.1 ▲　SO Site of the Wifley Mill site on hillside to the right.

▼ 1.0　SO Cross Southwest #7: Arrastra Gulch Trail. Pass under the Mayflower tram lines. Zero trip meter.

0.0 ▲　Proceed along the river road on the south side of Arrastra Gulch Trail.

GPS: N 37°49.65′ W 107°37.55′

▼ 0.0　Continue along the river road on the north side of Arrastra Gulch Trail.

1.6 ▲　SO Pass under the Mayflower tram lines. Then cross Southwest #7: Arrastra Gulch Trail. Zero trip meter.

▼ 0.4　Ruins of tram stands are visible on the mountainside across the river. Foundation and timbers on the left are

SW Trail #8: Silverton Northern Railroad Grade

from the Contention Mill.

1.2 ▲　SO Foundation and timbers from the Contention Mill on right. Then tram stand ruins are on mountainside across the river.

▼ 0.5　SO Remains of a swing bridge (cables and occasional timbers) cross overhead. Then timbers and a decaying structure are evident high on the valley wall, which were part of a wooden flume.

1.1 ▲　SO Timbers and a decaying structure are part of a wooden flume across the river, high on the valley wall. Then remains of a swing bridge (cables and occasional timbers) cross overhead.

▼ 1.6　End at intersection with Southwest #6: Silverton to Animas Forks Ghost Town road (County 110), just south of Howardsville.

0.0 ▲　From Southwest #6: Silverton to Animas Forks Ghost Town road at the southern side of Howardsville, zero trip meter at the bridge over the Animas River and turn onto a small trail marked "Private Property-stay on road" and proceed south.

GPS: N 37°50.08' W 107°35.95'

Maggie Gulch Trail

STARTING POINT Intersection of Southwest #6: Silverton to Animas Forks Ghost Town road and FR 588 at the town site of Middleton

FINISHING POINT Intersection Mill

TOTAL MILEAGE 4.1 miles (one-way)

UNPAVED MILEAGE 4.1 miles

DRIVING TIME 1 hour

ROUTE ELEVATION 9,800 to 11,900 feet

USUALLY OPEN June to October

DIFFICULTY RATING 3

SCENIC RATING 8

Special Attractions

- Varied, easy and scenic side road.
- Numerous mining remains.

History

At the beginning of this trail is the town site of Middleton. The town was named for Middle Mountain, which in turn got its name because it was located midway between Howardsville and Eureka. There were as many as a hundred claims being worked in the area in the 1890s. The town was formed in 1894, the year after the first mine was discovered. The town never amounted to much and many of the residents relocated to Howardsville or Eureka.

Maggie Gulch still contains plenty of evidence of early mining activity. The structures from the Ridgeway tramway were used to bring ore from the Ridgway Mine located some 2,000 feet higher. It carried the ore nearly a mile to the floor of the gulch for carting to the railroad.

Further along, above and to the left of the road, is the Little Maud Mine, which was worked from the 1890s with intermittent success. The washed out road that crosses Maggie Creek leads to the Empire Mine, a product of mining activity in recent times.

The Intersection Mine and Mill date back to around 1900. Much of the mill machinery is still located at the site. The mines above this site, along the hiking trail, were also part of this operation.

Description

This trail starts at the town site of Middleton. Nothing remains today but a new public toilet is located at the site. The road forks almost immediately and you bear left up a straightforward shelf road, switchbacking up the mountain. The right-hand fork is a short road that leads to several backcountry camping spots.

As the road climbs, it affords a good view along the gulch. You travel along a fairly wide shelf that is lined with pine and aspen. At this stage, the route is easy with a smooth, sound surface and adequate places to pass any oncoming vehicles.

After less than a mile, you have climbed almost 1,000 feet and the scenery changes dramatically as you emerge above the timberline

Intersection Mill at the top of Maggie Gulch

A section of road that cuts across an expansive talus slope

to cross an expansive talus slope. The aspen in the gulch below provide a particularly scenic view in the fall. The Ridgeway Mine tram is also evident in the valley.

The route then crosses a short, narrow section of shelf road as you pass a scenic waterfall at the top of the gulch. The scenery changes again as you enter a broad alpine basin and proceed along the last stage of the journey ending at the Intersection Mill. There are extensive ruins of the mill and its machinery, which operated in the early 1900s. At this point, the road contracts to a hiking trail, which continues to the Continental Divide, crossing it about three-quarters of a mile northeast of Stony Pass.

Current Road Condition Information

Silverton Chamber of Commerce
414 Greene Street
Silverton, CO 81433
(970) 387-5654

Map References

USFS   Uncompahgre NF or San Juan NF
USGS   San Juan County
Trails Illustrated, #141
The Roads of Colorado, p. 131
Colorado Atlas & Gazetteer, p. 77

Route Directions

▼ 0.0   From Southwest #6: Silverton to Animas Forks Ghost Town road in Middleton, zero trip meter and proceed east on FR 588 toward Maggie Gulch. The road immediately forks, so bear left and proceed up hill.
         GPS: N 37°51.30′ W 107°34.30′

▼ 0.9 SO Track on left.
▼ 1.1 SO Attractive view of waterfall at head of gulch.
▼ 1.2 BL Track on the right goes across the gulch to the Ruby Mine.

SW Trail #9: Maggie Gulch Trail

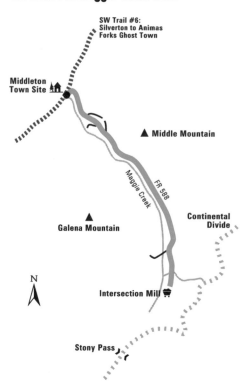

▼ 1.6   SO Track enters on left.
▼ 3.0   SO Track on left to the Little Maud Mine.
▼ 3.7   BL Road forks. To the right it crosses Maggie
            Creek and leads to the Empire Mine, but
            the bridge has been washed out.
            GPS: N 37°49.14′ W 107°32.12′

▼ 3.9   SO Cross through creek.
▼ 4.1   SO Cross through creek.
▼ 4.1   End at Intersection Mill with plenty of
            room to turn around.
            GPS: N 37°48.85′ W 107°32.14′

Minnie Gulch Trail

STARTING POINT Intersection with Southwest
#6: Silverton to Animas Forks Ghost Town
road and FR 587
FINISHING POINT Kittimac Mine
TOTAL MILEAGE 3.9 miles (one-way)
UNPAVED MILEAGE 3.9 miles
DRIVING TIME 1 hour
ROUTE ELEVATION 9,800 to 11,800 feet
USUALLY OPEN June to October
DIFFICULTY RATING 4
SCENIC RATING 8

Special Attractions
■ Historic mining district with many, well-
preserved buildings.
■ Moderately difficult trail with good
scenery.

History
The Caledonia Mine was discovered in 1872
and the Caledonia Mill was built in the early
1900s to treat ore produced at the Caledonia

Caledonia Mine buildings

Mine located 1,200 feet higher, half a mile northeast. The stone foundations of the mill are clearly visible stretching up the hillside. The remains of the tram that brought ore down to the mill are also visible above the mill. Shortly past the mill are the remains of three buildings. On the right-hand side of the road is the mill superintendent's house and on the left, the larger building is the boardinghouse for the mill workers. Both these buildings are well preserved.

Near the end of this trail is the Kittimac Mine, which may have been part of the same discovery as the Caledonia Mine in 1872. A tramway was constructed around 1900 to carry ore from the mine to the new Kittimac Mill built beside the Silverton Northern Railroad tracks next to the Animas River. The tramway was nearly two miles long and descended nearly 2,000 feet.

The Esmerelda Mine operated at its peak in the early 1900s and continued to operate for many years. Its longevity was due to the production of high assays of both silver and gold.

Description

This route heads east from Southwest #6: Silverton to Animas Forks Ghost Town road, initially traveling through the forest beside Minnie Creek. A little over a mile from the start is the site of the Caledonia Mill on the left, across Minnie Creek.

Continuing along the route you come to a fork in the road; both legs of this fork are included in this route. The left-hand fork is explored first. This road switchbacks up the mountain and although it is narrow, the surface is sound. You pass a tram support for the Kittimac Mine tram that transported to the Kittimac Mill located on the Animas River, just south of the start of this 4WD trail.

Farther along is the Caledonia Mine boardinghouse and stables. The boardinghouse is leaning at a precarious angle, only saved from collapse by the supports that have been put in place. The road continues to the Caledonia and Kittimac mines. As it does, it gets narrower and steeper. Turn at an appropriate place and head back down to the fork in the road to explore the other leg,

The miner's boardinghouse near the site of the Caledonia Mill

which leads to the Esmerelda Mine.

Once on the right-hand fork, the road heads farther up Minnie Gulch traveling above the creek. It passes two cabins, a waterfall from a side creek, and another cabin with a stone foundation—all on the left side of the road. The road gets more difficult as you travel along this last section, so turn whenever you think conditions warrant and return to the beginning of the trail.

The difficulty rating for this trail reflects conditions at the upper reaches of both forks. The earlier stages are quite easy. The varied scenery and the numerous mining remains make this short trail well worth doing.

Current Road Condition Information

Silverton Chamber of Commerce
414 Greene Street
Silverton, CO 81433
(970) 387-5654

Map References

USFS Uncompahgre NF or San Juan NF
USGS San Juan County
Trails Illustrated, #141
The Roads of Colorado, p. 131
Colorado Atlas & Gazetteer, p. 77

Route Directions

▼ 0.0   From Southwest #6: Silverton to
            Animas Forks Ghost Town road
            (County 110), zero trip meter and pro-

SW Trail #10: Minnie Gulch Trail

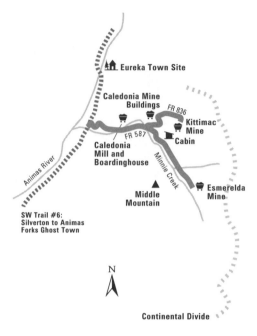

Eureka Town Site

Caledonia Mine Buildings

FR 836

Kittimac Mine

FR 587

Cabin

Caledonia Mill and Boardinghouse

Animas River

Minnie Creek

Middle Mountain

Esmerelda Mine

SW Trail #6:
Silverton to Animas
Forks Ghost Town

N

Continental Divide

ceed east along FR 587 toward Minnie Gulch. This intersection is about 6.6 miles from Silverton City Hall.
GPS: N 37°51.77′ W 107°34.07′

▼ 1.0   SO   Cross over Minnie Creek.

▼ 1.1   SO   Stone foundation from the Caledonia Mill on left across the creek.

▼ 1.2   SO   Building on the right; then two on the left. The large, well-preserved structure on the left was the Caledonia Mill boardinghouse.
GPS: N 37°51.48′ W 107°33.06′

▼ 1.4   BL   Cross over creek; then zero trip meter and bear left at the intersection. This route will later return to explore the track on the right, which goes to the Esmerelda Mine.
GPS: N 37°51.27′ W 107°32.27′

▼ 0.0   Proceed uphill.

▼ 0.2   SO   Kittimac Mine tram structure on left.

▼ 0.7   SO   At switchback, proceed toward the well-preserved Caledonia Mine board-inghouse and ruins of a stable. From

these buildings, turn around and continue up the mountain.

▼ 0.9   SO   Caledonia Mine on left.

▼ 1.0   BR   Track on left; then end at the Kittimac Mine a short distance farther. From here, the route directions will return to complete the fork that was passed earlier.
GPS: N 37°51.93′ W 107°32.22′

Continuation from the fork in the road

▼ 0.0   Zero trip meter at fork in the road. Turn left to continue along the other leg towards the Esmerelda Mine.
GPS: N 37°51.27′ W 107°32.27′

▼ 1.6   SO   Two cabins on left.

▼ 2.2   SO   Cross through creek with waterfall on left.
GPS: N 37°51.26′ W 107°32.26′

▼ 2.6   SO   Cabin ruins with stone foundation on left.

▼ 2.7   SO   Esmerelda Mine tramway ruins on right.
End of trail.
GPS: N 37°50.90′ W 107°31.94′

Eureka Gulch Trail

STARTING POINT Intersection with Southwest #6: Silverton to Animas Forks Ghost Town road

FINISHING POINT Sunnyside Mine at Lake Emma (drained)

TOTAL MILEAGE 3.6 miles (one-way)

UNPAVED MILEAGE 3.6 miles

DRIVING TIME 1/2 hour

ROUTE ELEVATION 10,000 to 12,100 feet

USUALLY OPEN June to October

DIFFICULTY RATING 3

SCENIC RATING 7

Special Attractions

- Visiting the location of the historic Sunnyside Mine.
- Lake Emma, accidentally drained in 1978.

An angle station for the Sunnyside tram on the hill beside the trail

History

This trail starts at the Sunnyside Mill at the town site of Eureka and finishes at the Sunnyside Mine, which provided the main economic support for the area. The Sunnyside Mine, located in 1873, became one of the best producers in the area. It operated continuously until 1931, when it shut down for a few years and then reopened in 1937. Two years later the miners went on strike, and since an agreement could not be reached, the mine was shut down again.

The first of the two Sunnyside Mills to be built in Eureka was opened in 1899, with a three-mile cable tramway connecting it to the mine. The second Sunnyside Mill, which incorporated much of the machinery from the Gold Prince Mill that that had operated at Animas Forks, began operations in 1918. It was built on the north side of the old mill. Eureka's mills also served the Toltec, Golden Fleece, Tom Moore, Silver Wing, and Sound Democrat mines. The mill was dismantled and sold for salvage in 1948.

Eureka, which had been founded in the early 1870s, flourished. The population reached two thousand, and the town had many stores, meat markets, saloons, and a restaurant. It was incorporated in 1883, making it one of only two incorporated towns in San Juan County (Silverton was the other). Eureka had its own post office, and a monthly newspaper, *The San Juan Expositor,* was published there. Otto Mears routed the Silverton Northern Railroad through the town in 1896, further strengthening the town's economy.

Toward the end of its operation, the Silverton Northern Railroad's steam engines were replaced by a combination of auto and locomotive parts called the Casey Jones, which could speed down the tracks between Silverton and Eureka in just twenty minutes. To clear snow off the tracks, the Casey Jones carried brooms strapped behind its

A close-up of the angle station ruins

cowcatcher. Service between Silverton and Eureka ended in 1939, and the railroad was sold and junked in 1942.

In 1976, the state of Colorado declared Eureka formally abandoned because it hadn't had a municipal government for the previous five years. Today, only a reconstructed two-story building stands on what was Eureka's flat town site. You also can still see the enormous skeleton of the second Sunnyside Mill.

As you drive up Eureka Gulch, there is much evidence of the mining activity that once existed. The Midway Mill, named for its location between the Sunnyside Mine and Eureka township, was built in 1890 and was connected to the Sunnyside Mine by a tramway. At the turn of the century, this tramway was extended to Eureka when the first Sunnyside Mill was opened. A second tramway was constructed in 1917 to service the new mill. The new tram incorporated some of the upper section of the old tramway, which brought its total length to three miles.

Continuing up Eureka Gulch, you pass a closed track on the left, which leads to the mile-long Terry Tunnel. Constructed in 1906, the tunnel was bored into the mountainside to connect with the Sunnyside vein.

One-half mile farther up the gulch is a large portal from the Ben Franklin Mine, which dates from the early 1870's

Many remnants of the Sunnyside tramway can be seen in the vicinity of the Sunnyside Mine. In 1888, a mill was built at the site of the mine but proved too expensive to operate. In the early 1900s, about as many as 200 men were employed at the mine. The Sunnyside Mine continued to operate on and off until fairly recent times. In the 1960s, it was still producing 600 tons of ore per day. The foundations of many of the buildings remain. Extensive reclamation work has been undertaken in the area in the 1990s.

The Sunnyside Mine buildings were clustered along the shore of Lake Emma. On Sunday, June 4, 1978, a tunnel that was being excavated about seventy feet under Lake Emma collapsed and completely drained the lake. Thousands of gallons of water and millions of tons of mud and rocks drained into the American Tunnel before exiting at Gladstone, some two miles away and 1,500 feet lower. The Terry Tunnel was also filled. The cleanup took more than two years to complete. Because the disaster occurred on a Sunday, the miners were not working and, fortunately, no one was killed.

Description

The route starts with a climb along a shelf road that is well maintained and reasonably wide with plenty of opportunities for passing. After about half a mile, the road levels off and continues along the wall of the gulch.

The route is simple to navigate and easy to drive. The scenery is attractive but the real attraction of the trail is its historical significance, evidence of which is abundant.

SW Trail #11: Eureka Gulch Trail

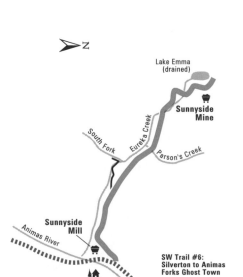

Current Road Condition Information
Silverton Chamber of Commerce
414 Greene Street
Silverton, CO 81433
(970) 387-5654

Map References
USFS Uncompahgre NF or San Juan NF
USGS San Juan County
Trails Illustrated, #141
The Roads of Colorado, p. 115
Colorado Atlas & Gazetteer, p. 77

Route Directions

▼ 0.0   From Southwest #6: Silverton to
         Animas Forks Ghost Town road (about
         0.3 miles north of Eureka), zero trip
         meter and turn onto Eureka Gulch Trail.
         Proceed up the hill.
         GPS: N 37°53.09' W 107°33.82'

▼ 0.4 SO Ruins of the second Sunnyside Mill are
           on left directly below road. On right is
           a tram structure that carried ore from

the mine to the mill, almost three miles.
▼ 0.7 BR Fork in road.
▼ 0.9 SO Snowslide defense structure beside
           the road on left and a private cabin on
           left across Eureka Creek.
▼ 1.0 SO Track on left to Midway Mill in the
           South Fork of Eureka Gulch.
▼ 1.8 SO Johnson Tower on left across the val-
           ley, halfway up mountain.
▼ 2.1 SO Cross over Parson's Creek with water-
           fall on right.
▼ 2.3 SO Tram tension station on left across val-
           ley on the mountain slope.
▼ 2.4 SO Track on left is gated and goes to the
           next entry.
▼ 2.5 SO Reclamation ponds on left for the Terry
           Tunnel.
▼ 2.7 SO Cross over Eureka Creek.
▼ 2.8 SO Large portal beside the road is from
           the Ben Franklin Mine.
▼ 2.9 BR Fork in the road.
▼ 3.0 BR Road joins on left.
▼ 3.3 SO Sunnyside Mine tram station on right.
▼ 3.4-3.6 SO Remains of mine buildings.
▼ 3.6 SO End at site of drained Lake Emma.
         GPS: N 37°54.17' W 107°36.86'

SOUTHWEST REGION TRAIL #12

California Gulch Trail

STARTING POINT Animas Forks
FINISHING POINT Intersection with Southwest
    #14: Silverton to Lake Como Trail
TOTAL MILEAGE 4.2 miles
UNPAVED MILEAGE 4.2 miles
DRIVING TIME 1 hour
ROUTE ELEVATION 11,400 to 12,930 feet
USUALLY OPEN June to late October
DIFFICULTY RATING 4
SCENIC RATING 9

Special Attractions
■ Spectacular scenery, especially the view
  from California Pass.
■ Many historic mining sites and structures.
■ A short, moderately easy 4WD trail.
■ Part of a large network of 4WD trails.

Lake Como viewed from California Pass

History

Numerous mines and mills operated in California Gulch and plenty of evidence of this activity remains today.

The Columbus Mine, located at the northern edge of Animas Forks, was discovered in the early 1880s. The mine yielded a large tonnage of ore, but it was low-grade

Bagley Mill

and high transportation costs meant that the mine was barely economic. As a producer of zinc, it had some of its best years during World War II. The mill, located at the mine, was built in 1927. The whole operation closed in 1948.

The Bagley Mill, built in 1912 to treat ore from Frisco Tunnel, was regarded as one of the best mills in the area; it had a capacity of 150 tons of ore a day. Construction on Frisco Tunnel, which burrows over a mile into Houghton Mountain, began in 1904 and took four years to complete. The mining operations ceased in about 1915.

About a mile farther is Vermilion Mine, which started operations in the early 1900s, with the mill being constructed in 1909.

Close to the pass as you climb out of the gulch is

Mountain Queen Mine, which was discovered in 1877 and operated until the 1940s. Rasmus Hanson owned the mine, and it has been speculated that Thomas Walsh managed it before he made his fortune from Camp Bird Mine.

Description

This route departs to the northwest of Animas Forks and is clearly marked to California Gulch. Traveling along California Gulch is a relatively easy road, entirely above timberline, with numerous mine remains and open mine portals in evidence.

The road ascends to California Pass, which provides a spectacular 180° view. It looks down onto Lake Como and Poughkeepsie Gulch, back to the road to Animas Forks, and across to Hurricane Pass and Hurricane Peak.

The section of the road descending from California Pass is the harder part of this route and traverses quite different terrain. There is a series of tight switchbacks along a narrow shelf road. At times, the road is steep, and passing other vehicles can be difficult.

The road is usually open from mid-June to late October, but snow often remains along the side of the road throughout the summer. This trail is likely to be muddy early in the season.

Current Road Condition Information

San Juan National Forest
701 Camino del Rio
Durango, CO 81301
(970) 247-4874

Silverton Chamber of Commerce
414 Greene Street
Silverton, CO 81433
(970) 387-5654

Map References

USFS Uncompahgre NF or Gunnison NF
USGS San Juan County
Trails Illustrated, #141
The Roads of Colorado, p. 115
Colorado Atlas & Gazetteer, p. 77

The Columbus Mill on the northern edge of Animas Forks

Route Directions

▼ 0.0   At the north end of Animas Forks, zero trip meter beside the bridge over the Animas River and proceed northwest (do not cross bridge), following signs to California Gulch. Cross over the West Fork of Animas River; pass the Columbus Mine and Mill on the right.
4.2 ▲   End at bridge in Animas Forks.
         GPS: N 37°55.89' W 107°34.22'

▼ 0.5   SO Bagley Mill and Frisco Tunnel on right.
3.6 ▲   SO Bagley Mill and Frisco Tunnel on left.

▼ 0.7   BL Track to Bagley Mill on right.
3.5 ▲   BR Track to Bagley Mill on left.

▼ 1.0   BR Southwest #13: Picayne Gulch and Placer Gulch Trail on left.
3.1 ▲   BL Southwest #13: Picayne Gulch and Placer Gulch Trail on right.

▼ 1.1   BR Track on left to cabin.
3.1 ▲   BL Track on right to cabin.

▼ 1.5   SO Vermilion Mine and Mill ruins on right.
2.7 ▲   SO Vermilion Mine and Mill ruins on left.

▼ 1.7   SO Burrows Mine ruins on right.
2.4 ▲   SO Burrows Mine ruins on left.

▼ 2.9   SO Cross over creek.
1.3 ▲   SO Cross over creek.

SW Trail #12: California Gulch Trail

SW Trail #5:
North Fork Cutoff

SW Trail #3:
Cinnamon Pass Road

Animas Forks Ghost Town

SW Trail #6:
Silverton to Animas
Forks Ghost Town

Poughkeepsie Gulch Road

California
Pass

SW Trail #13:
Picayne Gulch and
Placer Gluch Trail

Lake Como

Lake Emma
(drained)

Hurricane
Pass

SW Trail #14:
Silverton to
Lake Como Trail

▼ 3.0　SO　Open mine portal on right side of road.
1.2 ▲　SO　Open mine portal on left side of road.

▼ 3.4　UT　Intersection.
0.8 ▲　UT　Intersection.

▼ 3.5　SO　Road on left.
0.7 ▲　BL　Fork in the road.

▼ 3.6　SO　Mountain Queen Mine on right.
0.6 ▲　SO　Mountain Queen Mine on left.

▼ 3.8　UT　Summit of California Pass. The lake
you look down upon is Lake Como.
0.4 ▲　UT　Summit of California Pass.
GPS: N 37°55.02' W 107°36.91'

▼ 4.2　　　End at intersection with Southwest
#14: Silverton to Lake Como Trail to
the left. Corkscrew Gulch.
Poughkeepsie Gulch and Lake Como
are 0.3 miles ahead.
GPS: N 37°55.26' W 107°37.26'

Picayne Gulch and Placer Gulch Trail

STARTING POINT Intersection with Southwest #12: California Gulch Trail

FINISHING POINT Intersection with Southwest #6: Silverton to Animas Forks Ghost Town road

TOTAL MILEAGE 6.2 miles

UNPAVED MILEAGE 6.2 miles

DRIVING TIME 1 hour

ROUTE ELEVATION 10,500 to 13,000 feet

USUALLY OPEN June to October

DIFFICULTY RATING 4

SCENIC RATING 8

Special Attractions

- Varied, scenic trail.
- Many interesting mining buildings and other mining structures.
- Abundant wildflowers in early summer.

History

At the start of the trail, remains of the Gold Prince Tramway are visible on the face of Treasure Mountain to the left. Built in 1905, the tramway ran a mile and a half from the mine at the top of the gulch down to the angle station at Treasure Mountain and then another three-quarters of a mile to the Gold Prince Mill in Animas Forks. The tram transported 50 tons of ore each hour.

About a mile further are the concrete foundations of the Mastodon Mill, which was constructed in the mid-1880s and treated ore from both the Mastodon and the Silver Queen Mines.

The Sound Democrat Mine was discovered in 1899. Initially, ore had to be transported to the mill constructed at the Sunnyside Mine. In 1906, the Sound Democrat Mill began operations and continued until 1914.

At the top of the gulch is the Gold Prince Mine, which had been known previously as the Sunnyside Extension and the Mountain

One of the buildings remaining from the Treasure Mountain Gold Mining Company

Pride. Nearby is the concrete foundation of the boardinghouse that housed 150 miners. Beside it is the tram tower used to unload supplies for the boardinghouse. The Gold Prince was discovered in 1874 and worked the same veins as the Sunnyside Mine located less than a mile to the southwest on the other side of Hanson Peak. Rasmus Hanson built the Hanson Mill in 1889 to process the ore. The mine was still being worked in the 1950s.

In the early 1900s, Treasure Mountain Gold Mining Company built the cluster of buildings you drive past in Picayne Gulch, which include a substantial boardinghouse. This mining company consolidated and worked some thirty claims in the area including the Golden Fleece, Scotia, and San Juan Queen. The tunnel near the buildings is the Santiago Tunnel, built in 1937.

Description

From the start of this route, the road immediately crosses the West Fork of the Animas River. The road continues into the gulch and travels above Placer Creek. The scenery in the gulch is treeless alpine tundra. The beauty of the open countryside is enhanced in the early summer by massive displays of wildflowers. Placer Gulch still holds much evidence of the mines, mills, and tramways that turned it into a hive of activity long ago.

The road to the Gold Prince Mine at the top of the gulch is the easier part of the trail and would only rate a 3 for difficulty. From the Gold Prince, the road switchbacks up to the ridge and crosses into Picayne Gulch. This segment is fairly steep but is quite wide; there are plenty of opportunities to pass oncoming vehicles. Once into Picayne Gulch you travel through broad, open meadows where flocks of sheep are left to graze in the summer. This section of road is cleared by snowplow at the start of the season and can be quite muddy when wet.

The road re-enters the forest and passes the cluster of buildings constructed by the Treasure Mountain Gold Mining Company. These include a substantial boardinghouse that had an adjoining bathroom with bath, toilet, and hot and cold running water. The bathroom was connected to the boardinghouse by an enclosed corridor.

The last section of the route is a narrow shelf road that descends to intersect with the Silverton to Animas Forks road. Passing opportunities are limited on this short section, but the surface is sound and it is not very difficult.

Current Road Condition Information

Silverton Chamber of Commerce
414 Greene Street
Silverton, CO 81433
(970) 387-5654

Map References

USFS Uncompahgre NF or San Juan NF
USGS San Juan County
Trails Illustrated, #141
The Roads of Colorado, p. 115
Colorado Atlas & Gazetteer, p. 77

Route Directions

▼ 0.0   From Southwest #12: California Gulch
           Trail (approximately 1 mile northwest
           of Animas Forks), zero trip meter at
           sign to Placer Gulch and proceed south
           toward Placer Gulch. Cross over the
           West Fork of the Animas River.
6.2 ▲   Cross over the West Fork of the
           Animas River and end at intersection
           with Southwest #12: California Gulch
           Trail. Animas Forks is approximately 1
           mile to the right.
           GPS: N 37°48.79' W 107°39.72'

SW Trail #13: Picayne Gulch and Placer Gulch Trail

SW Trail #12: California Gulch Trail
SW Trail #3: Cinnamon Pass Trail
Animas Forks Ghost Town
Gold Prince Mine
Treasure Mountain
Hanson Peak
Treasure Mountain Mine Buildings
Eureka Mountain
N
SW Trail #6: Silverton to Animas Forks Ghost Town

▼ 0.1   SO Mine ruins on left directly below road.
6.1 ▲   SO Mine ruins on right directly below
               road.

▼ 1.1   SO Concrete foundations of Mastodon Mill
               on left.
5.1 ▲   SO Concrete foundations of Mastodon Mill
               on right.

▼ 1.3   SO Red-roofed mill on left across river is
               the Sound Democrat Mill.
4.9 ▲   SO Red-roofed mill on left across river is
               the Sound Democrat Mill.

▼ 1.5   SO Two standing tram supports on left.
4.7 ▲   SO Two standing tram supports on right.

▼ 1.6   SO Concrete foundation for Gold Prince
               boardinghouse on left with tram
               tower beside it. Mine building on
               right.
4.6 ▲   SO Concrete foundation for Gold Prince
               boardinghouse on right with tram
               tower beside it. Mine building on left.

▼ 1.7   SO Track on left; then cross creek. Shortly
               after, ruins of the Sunnyside Mine
               Extension/Gold Prince Mine structure
               on right.
4.5 ▲   SO Mine ruins of the Sunnyside Mine
               Extension/Gold Prince Mine structure
               on left. Cross creek; then track on
               right.

▼ 1.8   UT Track on left to Hidden Treasure, Silver
               Queen and Sound Democrat Mines.
4.4 ▲   UT Track on right to Hidden Treasure,
               Silver Queen and Sound Democrat
               Mines.

▼ 2.7   BL Tracks on right to scenic overlook.
3.5 ▲   SO Tracks on left to scenic overlook.

▼ 2.9   SO View to the Sound Democrat Mill in
               the gulch below on left.
3.3 ▲   SO View to the Sound Democrat Mill in
               the gulch below on right.

▼ 3.8   SO Faint track on right.

2.4 ▲	SO	Faint track on left.

▼ 4.1	SO	Short access track on left to ruins from Golden Fleece and Scotia Mines.
2.1 ▲	SO	Short access track on right to ruins from Golden Fleece and Scotia Mines.

▼ 4.3	SO	Open mine portal on left.
1.9 ▲	SO	Open mine portal on right.

▼ 4.5	SO	View across the valley to the southeast is Burns Gulch Trail.
1.7 ▲	SO	View across the valley behind you to the southeast is Burns Gulch Trail.

▼ 4.9	SO	Treasure Mountain Gold Mining Company buildings and mine on right; then track on right goes into Upper Picayne Basin.
1.3 ▲	SO	Track on left goes into Upper Picayne Basin; then Treasure Mountain Gold Mining Company buildings and mine on left.

▼ 5.0	SO	Open mine portals on right.
1.2 ▲	SO	Open mine portals on left.

▼ 5.2	SO	Treasure Mountain Gold Mining Company buildings on right.
1.0 ▲	BR	Treasure Mountain Gold Mining Company buildings on left.

▼ 5.8	SO	Track on right to the Toltec Mine.
0.4 ▲	BR	Track on left to the Toltec Mine.

▼ 6.0	SO	Open mine portal on left.
0.2 ▲	SO	Open mine portal on right.

▼ 6.2		End at intersection with Southwest #6: Silverton to Animas Forks Ghost Town road.
0.0 ▲		From Southwest #6: Silverton to Animas Forks Ghost Town road (approximately 1.5 miles south of Animas Forks and 2.8 miles north of Eureka), zero trip meter and turn onto track to Picayune Gulch.
		GPS: N 37°54.99' W 107°33.45'

Silverton to Lake Como Trail

STARTING POINT Silverton

FINISHING POINT Intersection with Southwest #12: California Gulch Trail near Lake Como

TOTAL MILEAGE 10.3 miles

UNPAVED MILEAGE 10.3 miles

DRIVING TIME 1 hour

ROUTE ELEVATION 9,200 to 12,400 feet

USUALLY OPEN Silverton to Gladstone: year-round. Gladstone to Lake Como: June to October

DIFFICULTY RATING 4

SCENIC RATING 10

Special Attractions

- Spectacular, rugged scenery.
- Beautiful Lake Como encircled by mountains.
- Numerous mining sites.
- Access to a network of other 4WD trails.

History

From Silverton to Gladstone, this route closely parallels the tracks laid by the Silverton, Gladstone & Northerly Railroad. In April 1899, the Gold King Mining Company established the railroad to reduce its freight costs to the new mill it was constructing in Gladstone. The train commenced operations on August 4 of that year. Then in 1910, Otto Mears leased the Gold King Mine and Mill operations and with it the Silverton, Gladstone & Northerly Railroad. In 1915, he purchased the railroad from the mine owners. The railway continued to operate until 1924 and was officially abandoned in 1937. The last of the tracks were torn up and sold for scrap during World War II.

About halfway along Cement Creek Valley (on the other side of the creek) is the site of the Boston and Silverton Mill, which had an output of 100 tons per day when it was built in the 1890s, making it one of the larger mining operations in the valley. A newer mill is built on the site of first mill. The Gold Hub Mining Company acquired the whole operation in the late 1930s. The Yukon Tunnel located just behind the mill continued to operate until the 1980s.

The Anglo-Saxon Mine, discovered in the late 1890s, was bought by the Gold King Mining Company; it produced tungsten used in the manufacture of bullet-proof steel during World War II.

On the left shortly after the road crosses to the east side of the creek is the Elk Mountain Mine, which operated for about twenty years before closing in the 1920s.

On the western edge of the town of Gladstone stand the foundations of the Mogul Mill, which was constructed in 1906 to treat ore from the Mogul Mine. It was connected to the Mogul Mine by a two-mile-long tramway.

Description

Navigating the route from Silverton to Gladstone, a well-maintained gravel road, is straightforward.

From the turnoff to Lake Como, just past the Mogul Mill foundations in Gladstone,

the road becomes much narrower and travels along a shelf above the North Fork of Cement Creek for about two and one-half miles. Although this section is much more difficult than the road between Silverton and Gladstone, the surface is quite sound, albeit bumpy, and the only real difficulty is negotiating your way past oncoming vehicles. As you travel along this shelf section, the 4WD trail to Mogul Mine can be seen to the east across the creek.

As you continue, you quickly climb above timberline; the scenery becomes much more rugged and offers some spectacular mountain views. There is a wonderful view of Lake Como and Poughkeepsie Gulch from near Hurricane Pass. Signs of mining activity abound along this route.

Current Road Condition Information

Silverton Chamber of Commerce
414 Greene Street
Silverton, CO 81433
(970) 387-5654

Map References

USFS Uncompahgre NF
USGS San Juan County
Trails Illustrated, #141
The Roads of Colorado, pp. 131, 115
Colorado Atlas & Gazetteer, pp. 76–77

Route Directions

▼ 0.0   From the Silverton City Hall at Greene (main) Street and 14th Street, zero trip meter and proceed northeast out of town.

6.5 ▲   End in front of the Silverton City Hall at Greene Street and 14th Street.
         GPS: N 37°48.79′ W 107°39.72′

▼ 0.2   SO Follow County 110 straight ahead. County 110 also turns to the right.

6.3 ▲   BR Proceed toward Silverton.

▼ 0.4   BL Hillside Cemetery is straight ahead.

6.1 ▲   BR Hillside Cemetery is to the left.

▼ 0.7   BR Track on left. Then cross over creek.

An old boiler located below Hurricane Pass

Lake Como and Poughkeepsie Gulch viewed from Hurricane Pass

5.8 ▲ BL Cross over creek. Then track on right.

▼ 1.0 SO Unpaved.
5.5 ▲ SO Paved.

▼ 2.5 SO Bridge over Cement Creek and track on left.
4.0 ▲S 0 Track on right and bridge over Cement Creek.

▼ 3.1 SO Boston and Silverton Mill site on the right. Newer buildings are part of the Gold Hub Mining Company.
3.4 ▲ SO Boston and Silverton Mill site on the left. Newer buildings are part of the Gold Hub Mining Company.

▼ 3.5 SO Track on left.
3.0 ▲ SO Track on right.

▼ 3.8 SO Logs and building behind it on left are remnants of the Anglo-Saxon mine.
2.7 ▲ SO Logs and building behind it on right are remnants of the Anglo-Saxon mine.

▼ 4.1 SO Bridge over Cement Creek.
2.3 ▲ SO Bridge over Cement Creek.

▼ 4.6 SO Cabin on left is part of the Elk Mountain Mine.
1.9 ▲ SO Cabin on right is part of the Elk Mountain Mine.

▼ 5.0 SO Cross over creek and railroad bed. Track on left goes through Georgia Gulch to the Kansas City Mine.
1.5 ▲ BL Track on right goes through Georgia Gulch to the Kansas City Mine. Cross over creek.

▼ 6.0 SO Southwest #15: Prospect Gulch Trail (County 35) on left.
0.5 ▲ SO Road on right is Southwest #15: Prospect Gulch Trail (County 35).
GPS: N 37°53.31' W 107°39.66'

▼ 6.5 SO Site of the Mogul Mill on left. Town site of Gladstone existed in the flat area to the right. Zero trip meter at the mill.

SW Trail #14: Silverton to Lake Como Trail

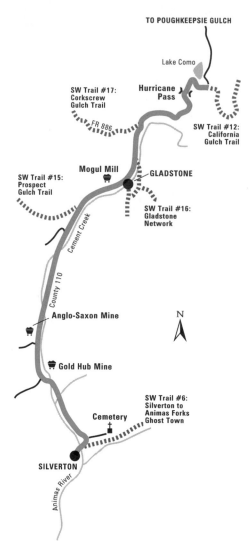

TO POUGHKEEPSIE GULCH

Lake Como

SW Trail #17:
Corkscrew
Gulch Trail

Hurricane
Pass

FR 886

SW Trail #12:
California
Gulch Trail

Mogul Mill

GLADSTONE

SW Trail #15:
Prospect
Gulch Trail

SW Trail #16:
Gladstone
Network

Cement Creek

County 110

Anglo-Saxon Mine

N

Gold Hub Mine

SW Trail #6:
Silverton to
Animas Forks
Ghost Town

Cemetery

SILVERTON

Animas River

0.0 ▲ Continue along track toward Silverton.
GPS: N 37°53.44' W 107°39.10'

▼ 0.0 Continue along main road.

1.5 ▲ SO Site of the Mogul Mill on right. Town site of Gladstone existed in the flat area to the left. Zero trip meter at the mill.

▼ 0.1 BL Turn onto County 10 towards Hurricane Pass, California Pass, and Corkscrew Gulch on left.

1.4 ▲ BR Onto Cement Creek Road.
GPS: N 37°53.46' W 107°38.99'

▼ 0.7 SO Track from the road to Mogul Mine joins in on right.

0.8 ▲ BR Road forks.

▼ 0.9 SO Track on right is private property to a modern cabin.

0.6 ▲ SO Track on left is private property to a modern cabin.

▼ 1.5 SO Southwest #17: Corkscrew Gulch Trail (County 11) on left goes to US 550. The road you can see in valley on right is Mogul Mine Road. Zero trip meter.

0.0 ▲ BL Proceed along County 10 toward Gladstone.
GPS: N 37°54.61' W 107°38.68'

▼ 0.0 Proceed toward Hurricane Pass

2.3 ▲ BL Southwest #17: Corkscrew Gulch Trail on right. Zero trip meter.

▼ 1.1 SO Lower Queen Anne Mine ruins on left.

1.2 ▲ SO Lower Queen Anne Mine ruins on right.

▼ 1.2 SO Track on right.

1.1 ▲ SO Track on left.

▼ 1.4 SO Mine on right is the Upper Queen Anne Mine.

0.9 ▲ SO Mine on left is the Upper Queen Anne Mine.

▼ 1.6 SO Open mine portal on left.

0.7 ▲ SO Open mine portal on right.

▼ 1.8 SO Hurricane Pass summit with a viewpoint on left down to Lake Como.

0.5 ▲ SO Summit of Hurricane Pass.
GPS: N 37°55.19' W 107°37.56'

▼ 2.3 End at intersection with Southwest #12: California Gulch Trail. Lake Como and Poughkeepsie Gulch are 0.3 miles to the left at GPS: N 37°55.41' W 107°37.38'.

0.0 ▲ From Southwest #12: California Gulch

Trail near Lake Como, zero trip meter at sign to Silverton and Corkscrew Gulch and proceed in that direction toward Hurricane Pass.

GPS: N 37°55.26' W 107°37.26'

Prospect Gulch Trail

STARTING POINT Intersection of Southwest #14: Silverton to Lake Como Trail and County 35

FINISHING POINT Galena Queen Mine

TOTAL MILEAGE 1.9 miles

UNPAVED MILEAGE 1.9 miles

DRIVING TIME 1/2 hour

ROUTE ELEVATION 10,600 to 11,900 feet

USUALLY OPEN June to October

DIFFICULTY RATING 3

SCENIC RATING 8

Special Attractions
- Numerous old mines.
- The remaining buildings and equipment at the Galena Queen Mine.

History
Prospect Gulch contains many mines dating back to early 1880s. The first major operation that you will see evidence of is the Henrietta Mine, which was discovered in the 1890s. Initially, ore produced at the mine was treated at the Fisher Mill in Gladstone. In the early 1900s, a mile-long tramway was built to transport the ore to the Silverton, Gladstone & Northerly Railway, which passed the entrance to this route as it headed up Cement Creek Valley. The railroad took the ore back down to Silverton for treatment.

At the top of the gulch is the Galena Queen Mine, established around 1890. It was only a small mining operation but continued in production into the early 1900s; much of the old machinery is still located at the site. Reclamation works are being undertaken in the vicinity.

Description
This route commences at the intersection of Southwest #14: Silverton to Lake Como Trail and County 35, about half a mile east of Gladstone. The entrance to this road is at the bottom of Dry Gulch. The road wraps around the southwest of the mountain before entering Prospect Gulch; from there it parallels the creek to the head of the gulch.

From the start of this route, the road ascends through the forest. The graded gravel surface is wide. The route is fairly easy to drive and very easy to navigate for the 1.9-mile route we have described. From there the road becomes much more difficult as it continues to climb Red Mountain; it is steep and narrow, and the surface is loose. Although we have not driven the whole way, we believe that the road does not go through.

Current Road Condition Information
Silverton Chamber of Commerce
414 Greene Street
Silverton, CO 81433
(970) 387-5654

Map References
USFS Uncompahgre NF or San Juan NF
USGS San Juan County
Trails Illustrated, #141
The Roads of Colorado, p. 115
Colorado Atlas & Gazetteer, p. 77

Machinery once used by the Galena Queen Mine

Route Directions

▼ 0.0   From Southwest #14: Silverton to Lake Como Trail (Cement Creek Road), zero trip meter at sign for County 35 and proceed up hill toward Prospect Gulch. This turnoff is about 6 miles north of Silverton and 0.5 miles south of Gladstone.
    GPS: N 37°53.31' W 107°39.66'

▼ 0.7 SO Old tram tower that serviced the Henrietta Mine on left.

▼ 1.0 SO Track on left to the Henrietta Mine.

▼ 1.1 SO Cabin on right.

▼ 1.2 SO Modern mine building on right.

▼ 1.3 BR Road forks. Left goes to the Crown Prince Mine.

▼ 1.4 SO John and Joe Mine and mine buildings on right.

▼ 1.7 BR Fork in the road. Left goes to the Henrietta Mine. Track on right goes up Red Mountain.
    GPS: N 37°53.46' W 107°41.13'

▼ 1.9   End at the Galena Queen Mine.
    GPS: N 37°53.52' W 107°41.35'

SW Trail #15: Prospect Gulch Trail

Gladstone Network

STARTING POINT Mogul Mill site in Gladstone
FINISHING POINT Mogul Mill site in Gladstone
TOTAL MILEAGE 11.8 miles (round trip)
UNPAVED MILEAGE 11.8 miles
DRIVING TIME 2 hours
ROUTE ELEVATION 10,800 to 11,800 feet
USUALLY OPEN Mid-June to early October
DIFFICULTY RATING 5
SCENIC RATING 9

Special Attractions

■ Network of short trails out of Gladstone.
■ Many old mines and mine buildings.
■ Wildflowers in spring and early summer.

History

This network of three trails commences from the mining town of Gladstone and explores the area in which the scores of mining claims were located that sustained the town's economy. Gladstone, founded in 1878, was named for the prime minister of Great Britain. The town got a post office that same year, which was to close three times in subsequent years as the town went through cycles of boom and bust. In its first year, the town also consisted of a general store, a meat market, a two-story hotel, a boardinghouse, and a small school house. There was also a newspaper: The Gladstone Kibosh.

Following the discovery of the Sampson Mine in 1882, development in the area started to accelerate. In 1887, the town was given its largest boost by Olaf Nelson's discovery of the Gold King Mine. With little capital, he worked the Gold King for three years until his death, and in 1894, Nelson's widow sold the mine for $15,000. Under the new owners the mine produced $1 million in gold, silver, and copper during the next three years. In the late 1890s, the Gold King Mill was constructed. The mill was expanded several times and at its peak produced 300 tons of treated ore per day. The

The Mogul Mill ruins, located at the western edge of Gladstone

The Lead Carbonate Mine produced good yields of both silver and gold after its discovery in the 1880s. It period of greatest activity was after World War II. A mill at the site was destroyed by a snowslide shortly after it was constructed in the 1930s. During its period of greatest production the ore was treated at the mill in Gladstone.

The Sampson Mine expanded its production following the completion of its mill near the North Fork of Cement Creek in about 1890. A tramway was constructed to haul the ore about two-thirds of a mile to the mill. In later years, the Sampson operation was amalgamated into the Gold King.

Along the third trail of this group, are a number of old mill ruins as well as the substantial Mogul Mine site. The Mogul Mine was discovered in the 1870s and a small mining camp was established at the mine. The mine tunneled nearly four miles into the mountain to connect with the Sunnyside Mine located at Lake Emma. From 1906, ore from the Mogul Mine was transported by a two-mile-long tramway to a new mill in Gladstone.

site of the Gold King Mill is now occupied by the steel mining buildings at the east end of Gladstone. Gladstone was the location of the outflow of mud and water from the collapse of Lake Emma in 1978 (refer to Southwest #11: Eureka Gulch Trail).

The Lead Carbonate Mill, located just behind the site of the Gold King Mill, was built in 1947 to process ore from the Lead Carbonate Mine in Minnehaha Basin about a mile away.

The first trail of this network goes to Colorado Basin, which was renamed Velocity Basin in the early 1990s when the world speed-skiing championships were held there. About a mile past the Lead Carbonate Mill are ruins from the Big Colorado Mine, which operated for about a decade from the mid-1890s. Storm Peak towers about 1,400 feet above the mine, recognizable by the microwave tower at its summit.

The second trail heads towards Minnehaha Basin, an area dotted by many many signs of the mining activity that was once abundant. The Minnehaha Mine was discovered in the 1880s and operated into the 1930s. The Black Hawk dates back the late 1890s.

The Mogul Mill and Gladstone circa 1940

The Lead Carbonate Mill today

Description

This route consists of three connecting trails extending from Gladstone: Colorado (Velocity) Basin, Minnehaha Basin, and Mogul Mine. The three roads split off from each other as the road winds around behind the metal building at the site of the Gold King Mill.

The Velocity Basin trail splits off first and follows the South Fork of Cement Creek. The first mile of the trail is through the forest traveling above the creek. Once above timberline, the scenery is majestic as you approach the end of the barren, gray, steeply sided basin. The road is moderately easy the entire way.

Returning to where the road to Velocity Basin split from the rest of the route, turn right and proceed north a short way to the turnoff, also to the right, that leads into Minnehaha Basin.

Minnehaha Basin is the location of the Minnehaha Mine, the Black Hawk Mine, and the Lead Carbonate Mine. This road affords some particularly good views, including across the South Fork of the Cement Creek Valley, Velocity Basin, and Minnehaha Basin. This trail has a length of

shelf road with a steep drop-off. However, the road is reasonably wide and there are adequate passing opportunities. The route ends shortly after the three deserted modern cabins, where there is plenty of room to turn around. The road continues past this point but is narrow and has been washed out before reaching the Sampson and Gold King Mines. Looking across to the mines, the Sampson is to the left and the upper Gold King is located to the right.

Returning to where the road to Minnehaha Basin split off, turn right and proceed toward Mogul Mine. This road is rough and rocky. Some of the rocks are quite sharp, so care is needed to minimize the risk of a punctured tire. From Mogul Mine, where we end the route, the trail gets very narrow as it goes higher into the upper Ross Basin. Even without proceeding into the upper part of the basin, this trail is the hardest of the three in the group and is the basis for the difficulty rating.

This network of trails offers an engaging mix of scenery: from spectacular, rugged mountains, protected valleys with swiftly flowing streams at their bases, steep-sided canyons, and many interesting remains from the bustling mine workings that once spread throughout the entire district. The numerous snowslide splitters are testament to the difficult winters endured by these miners.

Current Road Condition Information

Silverton Chamber of Commerce
414 Greene Street
Silverton, CO 81433
(970) 387-5654

Map References

USFS Uncompahgre NF
USGS San Juan County
Trails Illustrated, #141
The Roads of Colorado, p. 115
Colorado Atlas & Gazetteer, p. 77

Route Directions

Section one: Colorado (Velocity) Basin

▼ 0.0   On Southwest #14: Silverton to Lake

SW Trail #16: Gladstone Network

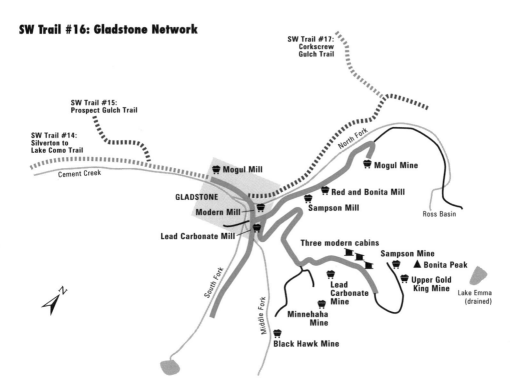

SW Trail #17: Corkscrew Gulch Trail

SW Trail #15: Prospect Gulch Trail

SW Trail #14: Silverton to Lake Como Trail

Cement Creek

North Fork

Mogul Mill

Mogul Mine

GLADSTONE

Red and Bonita Mill

Modern Mill

Sampson Mill

Ross Basin

Lead Carbonate Mill

Three modern cabins

Sampson Mine

▲ Bonita Peak

Upper Gold King Mine

Lake Emma (drained)

South Fork

Lead Carbonate Mine

Middle Fork

Minnehaha Mine

Black Hawk Mine

Storm Peak ▲

Como Trail at the Mogul Mill ruins along in Gladstone, zero trip meter and proceed toward the modern mining buildings.

GPS: N 37°53.44' W 107°39.10'

▼ 0.1 BR Southwest #14: Silverton to Lake Como Trail (County 10) forks off to the left.

▼ 0.2 TL/TR As you approach the Lead Carbonate Mill ruins, turn left and then immediately turn right. Note: You will return to this intersection to continue along the road to the left after completing the segment of the route into Colorado (Velocity) Basin.

▼ 0.4 SO Cabin on left.

▼ 0.5 SO Cross over creek.

▼ 0.6 SO Private track on left.

▼ 1.1 SO Big Colorado Mine on right.

▼ 1.2 SO Open mine portal on left. Then cross over creek.

▼ 1.5 SO Cross through creek.

▼ 1.7 End in steep-sided basin. Return to the

intersection at the 0.2-mile point above.

GPS: N 37°52.14' W 107°38.65'

Section Two: Minnehaha Basin

▼ 0.0 BR When you return to the intersection where you split off to go to Colorado (Velocity) Basin, bear to the right of the modern mine entrance and go past the Lead Carbonate Mill on the right. Zero trip meter.

▼ 0.1 TR At the next intersection turn right to head toward Minnehaha Basin. Note: You will return to this intersection to continue along the road to Mogul Mine to complete this network of trails.

▼ 1.4 TR Track straight ahead leads to the Gold King Mine. Follow switchback to the right.

▼ 2.0 TL Straight ahead about a hundred yards is a fork in the road. The left fork goes to Minnehaha Mine. The right fork goes to Black Hawk Mine and some private lots—it dead-ends in approximately one mile.

▼ 2.2   SO   Eastern Star Road on left is gated. Track on right goes to two modern cabins.

▼ 2.4   BL   Lead Carbonate Mine on right.
GPS: N 37°53.51' W 107°37.98'

▼ 2.6   SO   Three deserted modern cabins on left.

▼ 2.7   End of track—it is washed out ahead. You can see an outcropping of quartz approximately 50 feet onward along the road. Return to the intersection where you started this section of the route.
GPS: N 37°53.56' W 107°37.98'

Section Three: Mogul Mine

▼ 0.0   TR   Zero your trip meter when you return to the intersection where you split off to go to Minnehaha Basin. Continue towards Mogul Mine.

▼ 0.2   SO   Faint track on right.

▼ 0.4   BR   Fork in road. Left fork crosses through creek and joins County 10 toward Hurricane Pass.

▼ 0.5   SO   Site of the Sampson Mill and faint track to it on right.

▼ 0.6   SO   Red and Bonita Mill site.

▼ 0.8   SO   Track on right.

▼ 0.9   SO   Snowslide defense structure on left.

▼ 1.0   SO   Track rejoins on right.

▼ 1.5   SO   Mogul Mine and dump on right.

▼ 1.6   End at entrance to Mogul Mine on right. Beyond this point, the road is too narrow for full-sized vehicles, so turning around here is advised. Return to Mogul Mill in Gladstone.
GPS: N 37°54.60' W 107°38.27'

Corkscrew Gulch Trail

STARTING POINT Intersection of US 550 and FR 886

FINISHING POINT Intersection with Southwest #14: Silverton to Lake Como Trail

TOTAL MILEAGE 4.8 miles

UNPAVED MILEAGE 4.8 miles

DRIVING TIME 1/2 hour

ROUTE ELEVATION 9,800 to 12,600 feet

USUALLY OPEN Mid-June to late October

DIFFICULTY RATING 4

SCENIC RATING 9

Special Attractions

■ Exceptional scenery, with panoramic views of the Red Mountain Peaks and the more-distant mountains both west and east of the trail.

■ Provides access to a large network of 4WD trails.

History

This route commences near the town site of Ironton, which was located at the southern end of the old tailings pond. The town was formed in 1883 as a tent colony following the mining craze around Red Mountain four years earlier. Ironton developed into a somewhat refined town. Some merchants of the better stores in Ouray and Silverton opened branches in Ironton. Ironton served as the residential center for workers in the nearby mines, such as the Yankee Girl and the Guston.

The town also served as an important stage and supply center for the region. Wagons arrived at regular intervals, and ore wagons headed out from the city continuously. When Otto Mears opened the Rainbow Route, extending his railroad from Silverton, over Red Mountain Pass, through to Ironton in 1889, the town had a grand welcoming celebration.

Prospectors found gold in nearby mountains, which helped create another rush. New mine shafts were drilled deeper into the mountains. The digging of deep mine shafts resulted in the discovery of underground water; unfortunately, the water was found to contain deadly sulfuric acid, which often ate through machinery, making equipment maintenance a constant and expensive endeavor.

The modest success of the gold mines was not sufficient for the town to ward off the impact of the silver crash of 1893, and

The unmarked entrance to Corkscrew Gulch Trail along US 550

most of Ironton's residents moved on to other areas. A few hardy residents remained until the early 1930s. Some old buildings are left in the area.

Description

This route is moderately difficult to drive because some sections of the road are rough, steep, and narrow, and there are several sharp switchbacks to negotiate. However, other than locating the start of the trail, which is unmarked, navigation is straightforward.

The route commences at the Idarado Mine tailing pond on US 550. Initially the road, which is unmarked but designated FR 886, travels through the forest as it starts the ascent into Corkscrew Gulch. Sections of the road surface are clay and become very boggy in wet conditions. After you cross a couple of shallow creeks, you encounter several switchbacks as the road climbs out of the gulch.

Once above timberline, you have a panoramic view of adjoining mountains and valleys, including the three Red Mountains. As the road starts to descend, you re-enter the forest. From the turnoff to Gray Copper Gulch, the road is quite steep immediately prior to coming to an end at the intersection with Southwest #14: Silverton to Lake Como Trail

Ironton, 1908

SW Trail #17: Corkscrew Gulch Trail

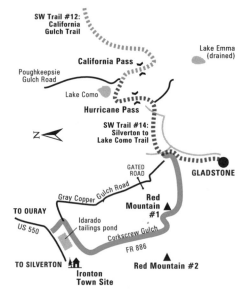

Current Road Condition Information
Uncompahgre National Forest
Ouray Ranger District
2505 South Townsend Avenue
Montrose, CO 81401
(970) 240-5300

Map References
USFS   Uncompahgre NF
USGS   Ouray County #2
Trails Illustrated, #141
The Roads of Colorado, p. 115
Colorado Atlas & Gazetteer, pp. 76–77

Route Directions

▼ 0.0   Begin at the sign for the Idarado Mine and its tailings on US 550. Zero trip meter and proceed east onto FR 886, crossing over plank bridge. This intersection is about 15 miles from Silverton and 7.7 miles from Ouray.

4.8 ▲   Cross plank bridge and end at US 550. Ouray is to the right and Silverton is to the left.

         GPS: N 37°56.33′ W 107°40.27′

▼ 0.2   BR   Sign indicates Brown Mountain left; Corkscrew Gulch right.
4.6 ▲   BL   Continue on trail.

▼ 0.3   SO   Sign reads "Corkscrew Gulch 4x4 only."
4.5 ▲   SO   Continue on trail.

▼ 0.6   SO   Track on right is the North Pipeline Trailhead.
4.2 ▲   SO   Track on left is the North Pipeline Trailhead.

▼ 1.1   SO   Track on left.
3.7 ▲   SO   Track on right.

▼ 1.5   SO   Track on left.
3.3 ▲   SO   Track on right.

▼ 1.6   SO   Cross through creek.
3.2 ▲   SO   Cross through creek.

▼ 2.0   SO   Cross through creek.
2.8 ▲   SO   Cross through creek.

▼ 2.7   BL   Cabin on right.
2.1 ▲   BR   Cabin on left.

▼ 2.8   SO   Sign to Gladstone and Silverton.

2.0 ▲   SO   Sign to US 550.

▼ 3.6   SO   Pond on left.
1.2 ▲   SO   Pond on right.

▼ 3.7   SO   Intersection.
1.1 ▲   SO   Intersection.

▼ 4.7   SO   Track on left to Gray Copper Gulch.
0.1 ▲   SO   Track on right to Gray Copper Gulch.

▼ 4.8   End at intersection with Southwest #14: Silverton to Lake Como Trail.

0.0 ▲   From Southwest #14: Silverton to Lake Como Trail (1.5 miles from Gladstone), zero trip meter and turn onto County 11 toward Corkscrew Gulch.

         GPS: N 37°54.61′ W 107°38.68′

Yankee Boy Basin Trail

STARTING POINT Ouray
FINISHING POINT Yankee Boy Basin
TOTAL MILEAGE 9.1 miles (one-way)
UNPAVED MILEAGE 8.6 miles
DRIVING TIME 1 hour
ROUTE ELEVATION 7,800 to 11,850 feet
USUALLY OPEN Mid-June to early October
DIFFICULTY RATING 3
SCENIC RATING 8

Special Attractions

- Historic mines and old mining camps.
- Canyon Creek shelf road.
- Abundant wildflowers in Yankee Boy Basin.

History

On the way to Yankee Boy Basin you pass the famous Camp Bird Mine. In 1896, Thomas Walsh, an Irishman, discovered very rich gold in Imogene Basin. He immediately purchased more than one hundred claims in the area and consolidated them under the name Camp Bird.

Camp Bird, a company town that grew up around the Camp Bird Mine, soon became the second largest gold producer in Colorado, turning out ore that was worth more than $1 million per year. The camp had its own post office, which was established in 1898 and discontinued in 1918.

Walsh furnished a boardinghouse for his employees with marble-topped lavatories, electric lights, steam heat, and even a piano. Meals were deliciously prepared and served on china plates.

Winter and snow were always problems for the community. The men often had to tunnel out of their quarters to reach the mine. Snowslides killed several men over the years. It was necessary to construct a two-mile aerial tramway from the mines to the mill. Camp Bird and the Tomboy Mine were linked by underground tunnels.

Six years after discovering the prosperous

Yankee Boy Basin

mine, millionaire Walsh sold the properties to an English company for $3.5 million cash, a half million in shares of stock, and royalties on future profits. Upon selling the mine, Walsh showed his appreciation to his employees by issuing bonus checks of up to $5,000.

With profits from Camp Bird, Walsh bought a mansion in Washington, D.C., and his wife and daughter hobnobbed with international society. They became "jet-setters" of their era. Walsh's daughter, Evalyn, married Edward B. McLean, whose family owned the *Washington Post*. As wedding gifts, each family gave the couple $100,000, which they supposedly spent before the

THE SILVER CRASH OF 1893

In the eighteenth century, currencies were typically backed by one or more precious metals. All major countries chose either gold or silver, or a combination of the two, as the basis of their currency. At the time, choice of currency was a major political issue both in Europe and in the United States; most countries changed their policy more than once during the course of the 1700s and 1800s.

Adherents of the system believed that it stabilized not only the prices of gold and silver but also the value of all commodities, thereby simplifying foreign exchange. Most economists came to oppose the practice.

In 1792, Secretary of the Treasury Alexander Hamilton led the U.S. Congress to adopt a bimetallic monetary standard, meaning that both gold and silver were used to back the currency. Silver dollars contained 371.25 grains, and gold dollars 24.75 grains—a 15:1 ratio.

One of the difficulties of this system is that as the relative market value of gold or silver changes, one coin becomes more valuable than the other; the more-valuable coin's circulation decreases as people melt it down and sell the metal and use the less-valuable coin for commerce. A metal's market value can change because of major discoveries of one of the metals or because one nation has changed its policy about the value of a metal backing its currency. In 1834, the United States was forced to change the gold content of its coins because France changed its policy. The U.S. ratio of silver to gold was increased to 16:1.

The Californian and Australian gold rushes in 1849 and 1850 resulted in a decline in the relative price of gold. The value of the silver in silver dollars became greater than the face value of the coins, resulting in widespread melting down of silver dollars. During the course of the Civil War, silver dollars disappeared from circulation; and in 1873, the United States moved to a gold standard, eliminating the free coinage of silver.

Subsequently, the large discoveries of silver in Colorado led to the price of silver falling below the old mint price, which created a political clamor for the government to revert to the old policy that supported the silver price. In 1878, Congress responded by reintroducing the minting of silver dollars but restricted silver purchases to between $2 million and $4 million per month. This was insufficient to quiet the clamor, and in 1890 Congress passed the Sherman Silver Purchase Act to provide for the purchase of $4.5 million per month. The result was an immediate increase in the price of silver from 84¢ to $1.50 per ounce, which had a dramatic effect on the silver miners in Colorado; times were booming.

However, the act caused the U.S. Treasury to start stocking silver bullion, since the value of silver decreased as increasing amounts were discovered. The government's stockpiling led to a lack of confidence in the currency and caused speculators to hoard gold, thus depleting U.S. reserves.

On August 7, 1893, President Cleveland called an emergency session of Congress and repealed the Sherman Act. The demand for silver was reduced by $4.5 million per month, and the price of silver crashed. Overnight, many Colorado mines became unprofitable and ceased operations. Populations moved, and many silver mining towns were doomed to become ghost towns.

In 1896, the presidential election was fought on the issue of gold versus silver. William Jennings Bryan supported silver, but William McKinley won. In 1900, McKinley succeeded in passing the Gold Standard Act, which led to further decline in the depressed silver price, more mine closures, and more ghost towns in the West.

In 1967, the United States eliminated the gold backing from the currency; by 1970, all silver content had been eliminated from U.S. coins, and the government sold the remaining silver reserves.

honeymoon was over. Evalyn Walsh McLean later purchased the famed Hope Diamond, which is now on display at the Smithsonian Institution.

The first cabin was built in Yankee Boy Basin during the winter of 1874–1875 when several prospectors endured the harsh, snowy winter. As the snow thawed, it was clear they had chosen a very successful locale for mining; they discovered both gold and silver and founded a mining camp called Porters. This was before Ouray was founded and several years prior to the first strikes at Camp Bird.

During the peak, as many as three thousand men worked the Yankee Boy Basin silver and gold mines. Sneffels served as the headquarters for local mines, although some smaller camps were situated around the more distant mines. Some of the profitable mines included the Yankee Boy, the Ruby Trust, the Wheel of Fortune, and the best producer of all, the Virginius Mine. In 1884, the Revenue Tunnel was constructed to intercept the Virginius at a cost of $600,000. The Virginius-Revenue project was so successful it paid for itself almost immediately and then, many times over.

A shelf road was cut into the mountain to Ouray, passing the future site of Camp Bird. The narrow ledges and steep grades were dangerous; rock slides and snowslides were frequent.

Although the silver crash of 1893 saw the closure of some local mines, rich ore and good management kept the Virginius open. Prospectors discovered additional gold veins. Operations were suspended in 1905 for some improvements to the mining works; but in 1906, a fire badly damaged the mine.

In 1909, operations resumed as normal; but the activity was short lived. When miners began sending their ores to the more economical Tomboy Mill on Imogene Pass, the Revenue Mill ceased operations. Ten years later, the mill was destroyed by fire.

The Sneffels post office closed down in 1930. The town experienced a brief revival during the late 1940s when some enterpris-

Camp Bird shelf road

ing folks rehabilitated several of the town's buildings and attempted to get the Revenue Tunnel operating again, but the town was never the same. The Revenue-Virginius properties later became the property of Camp Bird.

Description

Yankee Boy Basin is a very popular location during the peak summer months for both sightseers and hikers.

It provides a short, varied 4WD trail that is a good introduction to four-wheel driving. It offers rugged scenery, historic mines, deserted town sites, and wonderful natural beauty, including alpine meadows that are covered with wildflowers in the late spring. About five miles from Ouray, the route offers a spectacular shelf road as you travel above Canyon Creek. The road is well maintained and relatively wide.

From Camp Bird, the route takes you through a fairly wide, flat valley to the Revenue Mine and Mill and the old mining

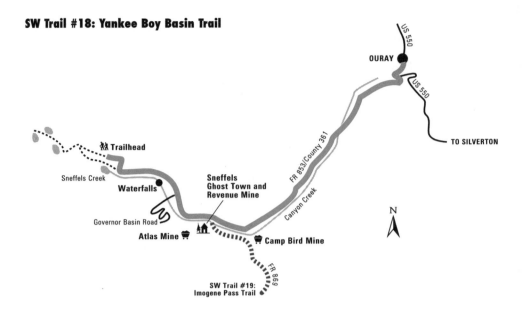

town of Sneffels, which can be viewed from the road but is on private property.

About half a mile further, the road forks, with the road to Governor Basin turning off to the left and the road to Yankee Boy Basin to the right. Until this point, the road is negotiable by passenger vehicles; further on it is for 4WD vehicles.

The Governor Basin 4WD trail is a narrow shelf road that is much more difficult than the Yankee Boy road. Passing is difficult in many sections, and snow can block the road late into summer, necessitating the sometimes difficult job of turning around. Nonetheless, for those with the experience and nerve, the Governor Basin road offers some majestic scenery and historic mines (difficulty rating: 5).

The road continuing into Yankee Boy Basin takes you past Twin Falls and numerous mines as you travel alongside Sneffels Creek to the end of the trail, some two miles further. Peaks ranging in height from Stony Mountain at 12,698 feet to Mount Sneffels at 14,150 feet surround the basin. The abundant wildflowers include columbine, bluebells, and Indian paintbrush.

There are numerous backcountry camping sites along this route, but camping is not permitted within a quarter mile of Sneffels Creek in Yankee Boy Basin and the tributary creek from Governor Basin. Also, camping is not allowed on private lands without written permission. Firewood is scarce in the basin, so if you are planning on camping, we recommend that you either bring some with you or use a gas stove.

Current Road Condition Information
Uncompahgre National Forest
Ouray Ranger District
2505 South Townsend Avenue
Montrose, CO 81401
(970) 240-5300

Map References
USFS Uncompahgre NF
USGS Ouray County #2
Trails Illustrated, #141
The Roads of Colorado, p. 115
Colorado Atlas & Gazetteer, pp. 66, 76

Route Directions

▼ 0.0 | In front of Beaumont Hotel at 5th Avenue and Main Street in Ouray, zero trip meter and proceed south out of town, remaining on US 550.

6.4 ▲ | End at Beaumont Hotel in Ouray at 5th Avenue and Main Street.

▼ 0.5 TR Toward Box Canyon Falls on Camp Bird Road, County 361.
5.9 ▲ TL On US 550 toward Ouray.

▼ 0.6 BL Box Canyon Falls on right. Bear left.
5.8 ▲ BR Box Canyon Falls on left. Bear right.

▼ 2.4 SO Bridge over Canyon Creek. Campsites.
4.0 ▲ SO Campsites. Bridge over Canyon Creek.

▼ 3.1 SO Camping on the left and right.
3.3 ▲ SO Camping on the left and right.
GPS: N 38°59.61' W 107°42.02'

▼ 3.3 SO Bridge over Weehawken Creek.
3.1 ▲ SO Bridge over Weehawken Creek.

▼ 5.0 SO Camping on the left and right.
1.4 ▲ SO Camping on the left and right.

▼ 5.1 SO Camp Bird Mine turnoff to the left.
1.3 ▲ SO Camp Bird Mine turnoff to the right.

▼ 5.7 SO Canyon wall dramatically overhangs the road.
0.7 ▲ SO Canyon wall dramatically overhangs the road.

▼ 6.2 SO Track on right.
0.2 ▲ SO Track on left.

▼ 6.4 SO Intersection. Southwest #19: Imogene Pass Trail on left. Track on right. Zero trip meter.
0.0 ▲ At intersection of Southwest #19: Imogene Pass Trail and Yankee Boy Basin Trail, zero trip meter and proceed northeast toward Ouray and US 550.
GPS: N 37°58.53' W 107°44.70'

▼ 0.0 Continue along road toward Yankee Boy Basin.

▼ 0.1 SO Road on right.

▼ 0.3 SO Revenue Mine and Sneffels site on left. Track on right.
▼ 0.5 SO Road on right.
▼ 0.7 BR Numerous campsites on left and right. Atlas Mine ruins on left across the river. Go past the information board.
GPS: N 37°58.67' W 107°45.36'

▼ 0.9 BR Road forks. Governor Basin road is to the left.
GPS: N 37°58.73' W 107°45.52'

▼ 1.2 SO Closed track on left.
▼ 1.3 SO Dual waterfall view on left.
▼ 1.5 SO Private road on left. Walker Ruby Mining.
▼ 1.6 SO Public restrooms on left.
▼ 1.7 SO Short road on left goes to a mine portal and then rejoins the main track.
▼ 1.9 SO Cross through creek. Yankee Boy Mine and tailing dump on right. Track on left rejoins from previous entry.
▼ 2.1 SO Tracks on left and right.
▼ 2.7 End of track.
GPS: N 37°59.45' W 107°46.76'

SOUTHWEST REGION TRAIL #19

Imogene Pass Trail

STARTING POINT Intersection with Southwest #18: Yankee Boy Basin Trail
FINISHING POINT Telluride
TOTAL MILEAGE 12.8 miles
UNPAVED MILEAGE 12.2 miles
DRIVING TIME 2 1/2 hours
ROUTE ELEVATION 9,000 to 13,114 feet
USUALLY OPEN Late June to late September
DIFFICULTY RATING 4
SCENIC RATING 10

Special Attractions

■ The highest pass road in the San Juan Mountains, with spectacular scenery and a wealth of historical interest.
■ The ghost town of Tomboy.
■ Views of Bridal Veil Falls and the switchbacks of Black Bear Pass Trail.

TELLURIDE

Telluride began as a small mining camp along the San Miguel River in 1878. The first residents called it Columbia. Because the post office sometimes confused Columbia with other towns of the same name, the town was renamed in 1881. Telluride, derived from tellurium (a metallic substance that is often attached to silver and gold in their natural states), was an apt name, since tellurium was widespread in the region.

Colorado Avenue in Telluride after a flood circa 1914

In 1881, business sites in Telluride were being sold for twenty-five dollars, and residential lots went for seventy-five cents. At this time, Telluride had a population of around a thousand people to patronize two grocery stores, and a whopping thirteen saloons! Two newspapers were established, and a school district was organized, with classes held in private homes. The following year, the townspeople raised funds to erect the first schoolhouse. The building still stands, but now it serves as Telluride's city hall. The first church, built in 1889, was followed by a number of others. One unconventional pastor even held services in a local saloon.

Telluride's mountains held fortunes in silver and gold. Zinc, copper, and lead were also mined in the area, but transporting the ores presented a major difficulty. At the Liberty Bell, miners tried to send ore from the mine to the mill downhill on sleds. This failed, because the ore kept falling off the sleds. The miners tried to steady the toboggans by constructing and adding wings, but too many sleds practically flew off the mountainside!

Telluride was isolated, so the townspeople often had trouble obtaining supplies and food. Lack of transportation also made shipping ore to Ouray on burros an arduous task. From Ouray, teams of oxen towed the ore to Alamosa. Finally, the ore traveled on to Denver by rail to reach the smelter.

When Otto Mears brought the Rio Grande Southern Railroad to Telluride in 1890, population growth was colossal, but little did people know what lay ahead of them. "To hell you ride!" the conductor would shout to passengers headed for Telluride.

History

The Imogene Pass road was built in 1880 to access Ouray from the Tomboy Mine. It was named for Imogene Richardson, the wife of one of Thomas Walsh's partners in the Camp Bird Mine. Wires carrying the first commercial transmission of alternating-current electricity were strung across this pass in the 1890s. The power was generated in Ames and transmitted to Ouray.

The Tomboy Mine, located in 1880 by Otis C. Thomas, was situated high above Telluride. Tomboy was Thomas's nickname. For several years there was little activity at Tomboy because it was so difficult to reach. However, after the silver crash in 1893,

prospectors struck gold at the Tomboy, and the mine began to produce handsomely. At its peak, the mining camp supported about nine hundred people.

In 1901, the Western Federation of Miners called their first strike in the Telluride area. This strike was successful, and non-union laborers were chased out of Tomboy over Imogene Pass. In 1903, the Tomboy Mill again began to use non-union labor, and a second strike was called. The mine owners asked Governor James Peabody to call out the state militia, and the governor, in turn, called on President Theodore Roosevelt to send federal troops. The U.S. army stayed away, but when five

Telluride was a wild place, where guns and tempers often got out of hand. The town's three dozen saloons and gambling halls never shut their doors. Telluride's saloon patrons seemed prone to drunken brawls and fights, and gun battles and murders were common. "The law" itself committed much of the lawlessness. Prostitutes were plentiful, especially along Pacific Avenue. The residents of town tolerated the prostitutes because the bordello madams paid all the town's taxes in regular installments on their behalf.

Butch Cassidy robbed his first bank in Telluride in 1889. Cassidy and two other men held up a bank at the corner of First and Colorado in broad daylight. Although they had three fresh horses waiting for them outside of town, they had no time to make the exchange as they rode for their lives toward Rico with the posse on their tails. Cassidy and his cohorts never were caught for the robbery, but several weeks later three dead horses were found still tied to the tree.

Set magnificently in a box canyon surrounded by snowy mountains and breathtaking waterfalls, Telluride has suffered problems from the elements. Historically, snow piling up in the mountain bowls has presented the greatest threat. In 1902, several men were swept away in an avalanche that also took out the Liberty Bell's tramway. More were killed when a slide buried the rescue party recovering the first bodies. The following day a third slide hit, bringing the death toll to nineteen. It took months to locate all the bodies. Two years later, nearly one hundred people lost their lives in snowslides. Floodwaters once washed out a dam on the San Miguel River, depositing up to eight feet of mud on the streets and isolating the town for weeks. To counteract this problem, residents constructed a flume leading from the town to the creek so that mud would wash into the creek, sometimes assisted by fire hoses.

Largely because of numerous complicated disputes between labor unions and mining companies, Telluride's economy declined dramatically in the early part of this century. One by one, the mines ceased operation. The most recent to close its doors was the Smuggler Union, renamed the Idarado in the 1970s.

Today, Telluride's gold is the ski industry, which started in the 1970s and has boomed ever since. Thanks to successful efforts at architectural preservation of Victorian houses and other buildings, the town looks much as it did a century ago. Telluride's community is currently prosperous and thriving with year-round resort activities.

hundred state troopers arrived, the violence soon escalated.

The union even brought in a hired gun, Harry Orchard, whom they had previously commissioned to assassinate the governor of Idaho. On union orders, he attempted to murder Governor Peabody, but the plot failed. With the area under military rule, the union and the strike were broken. The union labor was run out of town but set up camp at Red Mountain and plotted to recapture Tomboy and Telluride. Fort Peabody was constructed at the top of the pass in 1903 to protect against such an attack. The attack never occurred.

Although Tomboy's residents relied on Telluride for supplies, they did not necessarily turn to Telluride for entertainment. About halfway between the Tomboy and the Smuggler Mine was a renegade district called The Jungle, offering a mix of brothels, poker dens, and saloons.

The Tomboy Mine was sold for $2 million to the Rothschilds of London in 1897 and continued to operate until 1927.

This route was reopened as a 4WD road in 1966, following the efforts of various 4WD clubs.

Description

Imogene Pass is the second highest pass road in the United States and provides a wonder-

Mining ruins at Tomboy

fully scenic route through the San Juan Mountains. The route passes two major mining camps: Camp Bird and Tomboy.

From the Yankee Boy Basin turnoff, the road deteriorates and becomes 4WD. The track passes through the forest and Imogene Creek Valley. There are a number of creek crossings as the track proceeds toward the pass, although none should prove to be any

Social Tunnel

problem for a 4WD. The road narrows for the final ascent to the pass, but there are adequate pull-offs available for passing.

About two miles from the pass, the track enters the ghost town of Tomboy, 2,880 feet above Telluride, three miles distant, with its numerous historic remains. Although the buildings of Tomboy continue to deteriorate from the onslaught of harsh weather, Tomboy remains one of the better ghost towns to explore; many of the foundations and some of the structures are clearly evident.

Some two miles past Tomboy, the road passes through Social Tunnel, a short passage through a rock outcrop that provides a popular photo opportunity. This point also provides spectacular views of the switchbacks on Black Bear Pass Trail (Southwest #22) and both Ingram Falls and Bridal Veil Falls.

Current Road Condition Information
Uncompahgre National Forest
Norwood Ranger District
1760 Grand Avenue
Norwood, CO 81423
(970) 327-4261

Map References
USFS Uncompahgre NF
USGS Ouray County #2
         San Miguel County #3
Trails Illustrated, #141
The Roads of Colorado, p. 115
Colorado Atlas & Gazetteer, p. 76

Route Directions

▼ 0.0   At intersection of Southwest #18: Yankee Boy Basin Trail and Imogene Pass Trail (FR 869), zero trip meter and proceed across bridge over Sneffels Creek. Track on right, bear left.

5.3 ▲   Track on left. Cross bridge over Sneffels Creek. End at intersection with Southwest #18: Yankee Boy Basin Trail.
         GPS: N 37°58.53' W 107°44.70'

▼ 0.2   SO Track on right—no access.

5.1 ▲ SO Track on left—no access.

▼ 0.4 SO Creek crossing.
4.9 ▲ SO Creek crossing.

▼ 0.8 SO Old cabin on left.
4.5 ▲ SO Old cabin on right.

▼ 1.2 BR Private road to Camp Bird Mine on left.
4.1 ▲ BL Private road to Camp Bird Mine on right.

▼ 1.5 SO Imogene Creek cascading down through valley on left.
3.8 ▲ SO Imogene Creek cascading down through valley on right.

▼ 1.9 SO Track on right. Old sign to Imogene Pass. Cross through Imogene Creek with cascade on left. Another track on right goes to an old log building and mine.
3.4 ▲ SO Track on left goes to an old log building and mine. Cross through Imogene Creek. Track on left.

▼ 2.0 SO Spectacular view of Imogene Creek cascading into valley.
3.3 ▲ SO Spectacular view of Imogene Creek cascading into valley.

▼ 2.3 SO Cross bridge over Imogene Creek. Track on left to Richmond Basin.
3.0 ▲ SO Track on right to Richmond Basin. Cross bridge over Imogene Creek.
   GPS: N 37°57.22′ W 107°43.45′

▼ 2.7 SO Track on right to buildings and mine. Cross through creek.
2.6 ▲ SO Cross through creek. Track on left to buildings and mine.

▼ 2.9 SO Track on right. Follow Imogene Pass sign.
2.4 ▲ SO Track on left.

▼ 3.0 BR Series of tracks; continue to the right.
2.3 ▲ SO Roads rejoin on the right.

▼ 3.1 SO Roads rejoin on the left.

SW Trail #19: Imogene Pass Trail

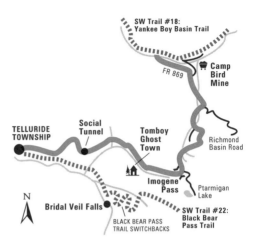

2.2 ▲ BL Roads on the right

▼ 4.1 SO Cross through creek.
1.2 ▲ SO Cross through creek.

▼ 4.4 SO Cross through creek.
0.9 ▲ SO Cross through creek.

▼ 5.2 BR Track on left to Ptarmigan Lake.
0.1 ▲ BL Track on right to Ptarmigan Lake.

▼ 5.3 SO Summit of Imogene Pass. Zero trip meter.
0.0 ▲ Continue along main road.
   GPS: N 37°55.88′ W 107°44.07′

▼ 0.0 Stay on main road and proceed downhill.
7.5 ▲ SO Summit of Imogene Pass. Zero trip meter.

▼ 1.2 SO Track on left. Stay on main road.
6.3 ▲ SO Track on right. Stay on main road.

▼ 1.4 SO Cross over drainage.
6.1 ▲ SO Cross over drainage.

▼ 1.5 SO Tracks on right.
6.0 ▲ SO Tracks on left.

▼ 1.7 SO Stone building remains on left.

5.8 ▲	SO	Stone building remains on right.

▼ 1.8	UT	Overlook of Tomboy mining township.
5.7 ▲	UT	Overlook of Tomboy mining township.

▼ 2.1	SO	Tomboy site.
5.4 ▲	SO	Tomboy site.

GPS: N 37°56.18′ W 107°45.23′

▼ 2.4	SO	Mill; then bridge over creek.
5.1 ▲	SO	Bridge over creek; then mill.

▼ 2.5	SO	Track on right.
5.0 ▲	SO	Track on left.

▼ 3.0	BR	Track on left.
4.5 ▲	BL	Track on right.

▼ 3.1	SO	Bridges over two creeks.
4.4 ▲	SO	Bridges over two creeks.

▼ 3.3	SO	Tomboy Mine remains.
4.2 ▲	SO	Tomboy Mine remains.

▼ 3.8	SO	Colorful mine buildings.
3.7 ▲	SO	Colorful mine buildings.

▼ 4.3	SO	Social Tunnel.
3.2 ▲	SO	Social Tunnel.

▼ 6.6	SO	Seasonal closure gate.
0.9 ▲	SO	Seasonal closure gate.

▼ 6.9	UT	Onto Gregory Avenue at intersection with North Oak. Then turn right onto North Fir.
0.5 ▲	TL	Onto Gregory Avenue. Then U-turn to the right at North Oak.

▼ 7.1	TR	Intersection of N. Fir and W. Colorado.
0.4 ▲	TL	Intersection of N. Fir and W. Colorado.

▼ 7.5		End at Visitor Information Center on W. Colorado in Telluride.
0.0 ▲		From Visitor Information Center on W. Colorado in Telluride, zero trip meter and proceed east on W. Colorado (main street).

GPS: N 37°56.37′ W 107°49.15′

Ophir Pass Trail

STARTING POINT Intersection of Colorado 145 and FR 630 south of Telluride

FINISHING POINT Intersection of FR 679 and US 550 between Ouray and Silverton

TOTAL MILEAGE 9.8 miles

UNPAVED MILEAGE 9.8 miles

DRIVING TIME 1 3/4 hours

ROUTE ELEVATION 9,500 to 11,789 feet

USUALLY OPEN Mid-June to October

DIFFICULTY RATING 3

SCENIC RATING 9

Special Attractions

■ Driving through the twenty-foot-high channel in the snow early in the season.

■ The long, narrow shelf road set into the talus slope on the west side of the pass.

■ Varied scenery, with exceptional views from near the summit toward the west.

History

This route was first called the Navajo Trail and was a well-used Indian hunting trail. The remains of an Indian camp were still visible near the pass in the 1880s.

Trappers were the first white men to use the pass. Explorers and prospectors followed them in the 1860s, and the road across the pass developed as a recognized route. In the mid-1870s after the Brunot Treaty opened up the region, a wagon road was built across the pass. The wagon road was converted into a toll road in 1880. When Otto Mears built his railroad through the area in 1891, the need for the pass road began to decline.

Throughout the mining period, the name Ophir referred to two towns near each other: Old Ophir and Ophir Loop. Located at the foot of Ophir Pass, Old Ophir, or just Ophir, was established in 1870, shortly before Ophir Loop. Early settlers named the towns after an Old Testament reference to a region rich in gold, in hopes that the nearby mines would bring similar fortunes. The first claims were staked in 1875, after which time prospectors worked the area sporadically.

By 1885, the population of Ophir grew to two hundred. In three years, it blossomed to five hundred. Ophir had five saloons, several churches, a school, and its own electricity and water works.

The town was often snowbound because of avalanches. In December 1883, a mail carrier named Swen Nilson left Silverton to deliver sixty pounds of Christmas packages and letters to Ophir and was never seen or heard from again. Although some people believed he had stolen the mail and fled the country, Swen's brother set out to search for him. After two years, he finally discovered Swen's skeleton with the mail sack still around his neck.

New Ophir, or Ophir Loop, was founded in the mid-1870s two miles from Ophir. Although a railway in this area seemed inconceivable, Otto Mears did not know the word impossible. Getting trains started up the steep grade to Lizard Head Pass was a true feat of railroad engineering. Mears oversaw the construction of three tiers of tracks with loops crossing above and below each other and trestles as high as one hundred feet. Over this incredible structure, the railroad ran from Telluride to Durango. Two cars of ore were shipped from Ophir Loop each day, and the town accumulated a small population as a few of Ophir's residents moved closer to the railroad.

The population of Ophir dwindled after

The Ophir Loop incorporating a large wooden trestle circa 1925

The Ophir Pass Trail in early June

the turn of the century, and the area was close to being a ghost town by 1929. In 1960, it was listed as one of four incorporated towns in the United States with no residents. However, the town is now home to a number of summer residents.

The current 4WD road was opened in 1953.

Description

The turnoff from Colorado 145 at the site of the Ophir Loop starts this track; but it is not well marked, so we recommend that you measure the distance from Telluride on your odometer. Those with GPS receivers will be glad to have the benefit of modern technology.

Across the highway from the start of this trail is a short road to the township of Ames, the site of the first commercial, alternating-current electricity generating plant in the United States.

As you leave the old township of Ophir, the road starts to ascend immediately through scenic woods and aspen stands. As the ascent continues, the road rises above the timberline and becomes a narrow shelf road cut into the talus slope with some tight switchbacks and high, steep drop-offs. This section is the most difficult part of the route. For a short section, passing requires

Mears's Million Dollar Highway in 1909

OTTO MEARS—"THE PATHFINDER OF THE SAN JUANS"

Otto Mears, born in Russia in 1840, was orphaned at the age of four. Various relatives took care of him, first in Russia, then in England, then in New York, and finally in San Francisco when he was twelve. When he arrived in San Francisco to live with an uncle, he found that the uncle had left for the gold rush in Australia; Mears was on his own.

He drifted through the mining camps of Nevada before serving in the First California Volunteers in the Civil War. From 1863–1864, he served under Kit Carson in the Indian Campaign against the Navajos. After the war, Mears first went to Santa Fe before moving to Colorado, where he opened a store in Saguache. He prospered and expanded his business interests. He farmed in the San Luis Valley and operated a sawmill and a grain mill.

To expand market access for his wheat, Mears constructed a road over Poncha Pass. The government gave permission for this road to become a toll road. Thus, Mears acquired the sobriquet Pathfinder of the San Juans. By the mid-1880s, Mears had built 450 miles of roads in the region. His most famous road is what has become known as the Million Dollar Highway, U.S. Highway 550 between Silverton and Ouray.

As the railroads expanded in Colorado, Mears naturally expanded his interests into railroad construction. In partnership with the Denver & Rio Grande Railroad, he built a network of four narrow-gauge rail lines. In 1887, he built the main line from Durango to Rico, over Lizard Head Pass on what is now Colorado Highway 145, descending with the aid of the Ophir Loop and proceeding to Placerville, Ridgeway, and south to Ouray.

Mears learned the Ute language and was friendly with Chief Ouray. He served as an interpreter in the Brunot Treaty negotiations. Following the Meeker Massacre, he assisted Chief Ouray in freeing the women captives. As a result, Mears worked with Ouray to negotiate the resulting Washington Treaty, which was signed in March 1880. In June, Mears was chosen by President Rutherford Hayes as one of five commissioners to implement the treaty. In 1884, he was elected to the Colorado legislature and became influential in the Republican Party.

Mears suffered heavily in the silver crash of 1893, with many of his enterprises being jeopardized or bankrupted. In 1907, Mears returned to Silverton and remained there until his retirement to Pasadena, California, in 1917. He died on June 24, 1931, at the age of ninety-one.

careful negotiation. Traveling slowly and carefully, moderately experienced drivers should not have any difficulty. The road is certainly easier than Southwest #22, Black Bear Pass Trail, but those who are tempted to take the route too lightly should heed the lesson offered by the remains of a wrecked vehicle that rolled off the road at this point.

From the summit of the pass to US 550, the route is much easier. Although the road is wider and the footing more sound, it remains a shelf road for much of the balance of the journey.

The varied scenery offers some particularly panoramic views on the west side. The east side is more heavily wooded than the west side, and the wildflowers in the valley add color.

The intersection with FR 820 offers an alternative route to US 550. The road, about 1.5 miles long, at times provides a challenging crossing through Mineral Creek. It joins US 550 0.7 miles north of where the main route intersects. Ouray is about eighteen miles north and Silverton five miles south of the intersection with US 550.

The road opens in early to mid-June each year. The snowplow only clears the east side of the pass to the summit. When the road is first opened, the plow leaves a narrow chan-

nel through the snow for 4WDs to travel—the sides are up to twenty feet high.

Current Road Condition Information
San Juan National Forest
701 Camino del Rio
Durango, CO 81301
(970) 247-4874

Map References
USFS Uncompahgre NF or San Juan NF
USGS San Miguel County #3
San Juan County
Trails Illustrated, #141
The Roads of Colorado, pp. 114–115
Colorado Atlas & Gazetteer, p. 76

Route Directions

▼ 0.0		At intersection of Colorado 145 and FR 630 at Ophir Loop (no signpost, but opposite the Ames turnoff), zero trip meter and turn onto FR 630 heading east toward Ophir. This is 10 miles from the Telluride Visitor Center.
5.7 ▲		End at intersection of Colorado 145 and FR 630 at Ophir Loop.
		GPS: N 37°51.74' W 107°52.11'

▼ 0.6	SO	Seasonal gate.
5.1 ▲	SO	Seasonal gate.

SW Trail #20: Ophir Pass Trail

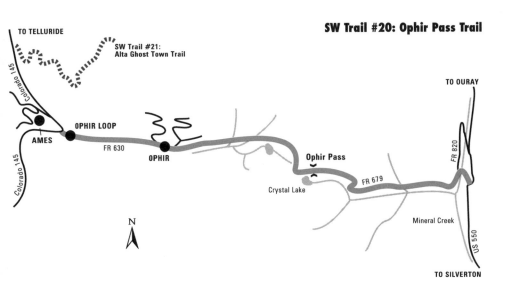

▼ 2.0   SO   Seasonal gate. Enter town of Ophir.
             Follow sign to Ophir Pass.
3.7 ▲   SO   Leave Ophir. Seasonal gate.

▼ 2.1   BR   Road forks. Then Ophir Pass sign.
3.6 ▲   BL   Road forks.

▼ 2.6 BL/TR Stay on main road.
3.1 ▲ TL/BR Stay on main road.

▼ 2.7   SO   Leaving town on Ophir Pass Trail.
3.0 ▲   SO   Enter Ophir town limits.

▼ 3.2   SO   Track on right.
2.4 ▲   SO   Track on left.

▼ 3.7   SO   Two tracks on left.
2.0 ▲   SO   Two tracks on right.

▼ 3.8   SO   Track on left.
1.9 ▲   SO   Track on right.

▼ 4.1   SO   Track on left.
1.6 ▲   SO   Track on right.

▼ 4.2   SO   Tracks on left and right. Track on right
             goes to the lake and campsites.
1.5 ▲   SO   Track on left goes to the lake and
             campsites. Tracks on right.

▼ 5.7   SO   Summit of Ophir Pass. Zero trip meter.
0.0 ▲   Continue along main track toward
             Ophir.
             GPS: N 37°51.00′ W 107°46.72′

▼ 0.0   Continue along main track.
4.1 ▲   SO   Summit of Ophir Pass. Zero trip meter.

▼ 0.5   SO   Tracks on left.
3.6 ▲   SO   Tracks on right.

▼ 1.0   UT   Track on left.
3.1 ▲   BL   Track on right.

▼ 3.2   SO   Track on right.
0.9 ▲   SO   Track on left.

▼ 3.7   SO   Columbine Lake Trail on left
             (FR 820).

0.4 ▲   SO   Columbine Lake Trail on right
             (FR 820).

▼ 3.9   SO   Cross bridge.
0.2 ▲   SO   Cross bridge.

▼ 4.1   End at intersection with US 550.
0.0 ▲   From intersection of US 550 and San
             Juan County 8 (FR 679), zero trip
             meter and proceed along County 8
             toward Ophir.
             GPS: N 37°50.84′ W 107°43.44′

SOUTHWEST REGION TRAIL #21

Alta Ghost Town Trail

STARTING POINT Telluride
FINISHING POINT Alta Lakes
TOTAL MILEAGE 12.4 miles (one-way)
UNPAVED MILEAGE 4.2 miles
DRIVING TIME 1 hour
ROUTE ELEVATION 9,700 to 11,100 feet
USUALLY OPEN Mid-June to October
DIFFICULTY RATING 2
SCENIC RATING 8

Special Attractions
■ Alta, a well-preserved ghost town.
■ The picturesque Alta Lakes.

History
Alta was the company town for the Gold
King Mine, which was discovered in 1878
and operated as recently as the 1940s. Gold,
silver, copper, and lead were mined and
transported in aerial tramcars from the Gold
King and other mines to the Ophir Loop,
two miles further down the mountain.

Alta's Gold King was a very rich mine,
but it was expensive to operate because of its
high altitude. Fortunately, L. L. Nunn
found a way to reduce expenses by bringing
electrical power to the mine. In 1881, he
organized a contract with the Westinghouse
company to construct an electrical plant in
Ames, less than three miles away. George
Westinghouse was a supporter of alternat-

Alta Lakes

ing-current electricity against the strong opposition of Thomas Edison.

The plant harnessed the power of the San Miguel River, transmitting 3,000 volts of alternating-current back up to the Gold King Mine. Encouraged by the success of this first alternating-current power transmission plant in America, Nunn expanded his venture to supply the city of Telluride, as well as many nearby mines, and installed transmission lines across Imogene Pass. Subsequently, electricity became widely used in Colorado and the world.

There were three mills at Alta, all of which have burned down. The last one burned in 1945 while seven men were underground. The superintendent ordered the portal to be dynamited in order to cut off the draft that was feeding the fire, even though his son was one of the men inside.

Due to the longevity of the Gold King Mine, Alta thrived longer than most high-country mining towns. Visitors can still see quite a few well-preserved old buildings, including a boardinghouse, cabins, and

A view of Alta in about 1895

some more substantial homes. Alta never had a church or a post office.

Description

FR 632, an unpaved road from Colorado 145 to the township of Alta, is well maintained and in good weather conditions can be traveled easily by passenger cars.

FR 632 meets Colorado 145 1.7 miles north of the intersection with the start of the road to Ophir Pass (Southwest #20). On the western side of Colorado 145 at the Ophir Pass turnoff is the road to the township of Ames, where the electricity for Alta was generated.

A short way above the Alta ghost town are the very scenic Alta Lakes, located at timberline. The lakes have good picnic facilities and public toilets.

The road to the lakes is also easy, but the road that encircles the lakes can be extremely rutted and muddy. This section of road would have a difficulty rating of 5.

A number of maps suggest that there is a road from the Alta Lakes to the Telluride ski area. However, when we were last there, this road had been blocked off. We were not able to confirm that this road would be reopened.

SW Trail #21: Alta Ghost Town Trail

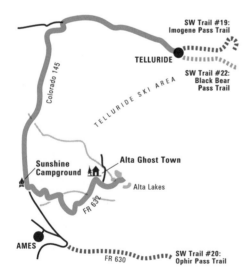

Current Road Condition Information

Uncompahgre National Forest
Norwood Ranger District
1760 Grand Avenue
Norwood, CO 81423
(970) 327-4261

Map References

USFS   Uncompahgre NF
USGS   San Miguel County #3
Trails Illustrated, #141
The Roads of Colorado, p. 114
Colorado Atlas & Gazetteer, p. 76

Route Directions

▼ 0.0		In front of the Telluride Visitor Information Center on W. Colorado in Telluride, zero trip meter and proceed west out of town. **GPS: N 37°56.37′ W 107°49.15′**

▼ 3.1	TL	Follow Colorado 145 south toward Ophir.
▼ 7.8	SO	Sunshine Campground on right.
▼ 8.2	TL	National Forest access sign on right (FR 632) toward Alta and Alta Lakes. Unpaved. Zero trip meter. **GPS: N 37°53.02′ W 107°53.25′**

▼ 0.0		Proceed toward Alta on FR 632.
▼ 2.9	SO	Track on right.
▼ 3.0	SO	Track on left with private property sign. Gate. Sign to stay on designated roads.
▼ 3.0	SO	Track on right.
▼ 3.4	SO	Private track on left. Private track on right.
▼ 3.7	BR	Ghost town of Alta. Zero trip meter at small sign for Alta Lakes. **GPS: N 37°53.13′ W 107°51.28′**

▼ 0.0		Follow track on right toward Alta Lakes.
▼ 0.3	BL	Road forks.
▼ 0.5		Road forks. End at Alta Lakes. There are numerous spots for picnics and tracks winding around the lakes. **GPS: N 37°52.83′ W 107°50.87′**

A view of the trail descending Black Bear Pass

Black Bear Pass Trail

STARTING POINT Ouray
FINISHING POINT Telluride
TOTAL MILEAGE 25.2 miles
UNPAVED MILEAGE 10.1 miles
DRIVING TIME 2 1/2 hours
ROUTE ELEVATION 9,000 to 12,840 feet
USUALLY OPEN Mid-July to late September
DIFFICULTY RATING 6
SCENIC RATING 10

Special Attractions

- Expansive views of Telluride, nestled in the valley four thousand feet below.
- Ingram Falls and Bridal Veil Falls, the highest waterfall in Colorado.
- The challenge of completing a difficult 4WD trail.

History

Black Bear Pass has also been known as Ingram Pass, after J. Ingram, who discovered the Smuggler Union Mine in 1876. Although Black Bear Pass is now the name commonly used, it has not been accepted by the U.S. Geological Survey Board on Geographical Names.

Black Bear Pass Trail was developed in the late 1800s to provide access to the Black Bear Mine. In the early 1900s, it fell into disrepair and was reopened as a 4WD road in 1959 through the efforts of the Telluride Jeep Club.

At 365 feet, Bridal Veil Falls is the highest waterfall in Colorado. On the canyon rim above the falls is a restored hydroelectric plant, built in 1904. Now a National Historic Landmark, it once generated power for nearby mines.

Description

The one-way Black Bear Pass Trail is one of the more difficult 4WD trails included in this book. It can be dangerous and has claimed many lives during the past thirty years. Just how difficult you will find it depends on your vehicle, your 4WD experience, and current road conditions. We have

View of Bridal Veil Falls and the switchbacks on Black Bear Pass 4WD trail looking from Imogene Pass Road

included it here for drivers who wish to try a more demanding road and because it is justly famous for its scenery.

The trail is not suitable for a full-sized vehicle, due to the very tight switchbacks on the steep, western side of the pass. It is the only trail in this book that we have never traveled in our Suburban. Taken slowly and carefully in a small vehicle, this pass should not be beyond the abilities of any driver who has comfortably undertaken a broad selection of the easier trails included in this book.

The portion of the trail that earns its difficulty rating stretches from the summit of the pass to the U-turn at the entrance to the power station at Bridal Veil Falls about four miles below. This section is one way and can only be traveled from east to west.

From the Million Dollar Highway, US 550, the road starts its climb toward the pass. About a mile before the summit of the pass, the road flattens out, leading through lovely meadows with little alpine lakes and waterfalls in beautiful tundra countryside.

At the summit, a network of tracks provides a multitude of wide, panoramic views. The abundance of tracks makes it difficult to identify the main track down to the west side; but by looking down into the valley (to the northwest of the summit), you can easily see the road you need to take.

Dropping down from the pass, the road heads into a treeless alpine valley but remains quite easy. The water crossings may be of concern to some drivers, but the base is sound and should pose little problem when taken carefully. Some slipping on the talus surface must be anticipated. Up to this point, the degree of difficulty would be rated at only 3. As you will have noticed, though, the spectacular views are already evident.

The road continues to get rougher and more difficult as you descend. Obstacles that may prove too challenging for inexperienced four-wheelers include tight, off-camber switchbacks, loose talus, and narrow shelf roads with thousand-foot-plus drop-offs. Because of the difficulty of this section of road, local 4WD rental businesses do not permit their vehicles to cross this pass.

The very tight switchbacks commence about two miles below the summit. The road has a formidable reputation, and when you get to these switchbacks, it is easy to see why. One switchback is particularly notorious and is justly considered impassable for full-sized vehicles. A short distance further, the road crosses the creek directly above Ingram Falls.

The route provides many scenic views of Bridal Veil Falls and the early hydroelectric power station. Numerous mines and tramways are evident during the journey down into Telluride.

We think this is one of the great 4WD roads of Colorado. Although experienced four-wheelers may not find it as difficult as it is reputed to be, we are sure they will consider it a great drive.

Current Road Condition Information
Uncompahgre National Forest
Norwood Ranger District
1760 Grand Avenue
Norwood, CO 81423
(970) 327-4261

Map References

USFS   Uncompahgre NF or San Juan NF
USGS   San Juan County
San Miguel County #3
Trails Illustrated, #141
The Roads of Colorado, pp. 114–115
Colorado Atlas & Gazetteer, p. 76

Route Directions

▼ 0.0   In front of Beaumont Hotel at 5th and
            Main in Ouray, zero trip meter and pro-
            ceed south out of town, remaining on
            US 550.
            GPS: N 38°01.30' W 107°40.29'

▼ 12.9 TR Onto Black Bear Pass Trail (FR 823), just
            beyond the summit marker of Red
            Mountain. Only a small, brown 4WD
            signpost marks the track. Zero trip meter.
            GPS: N 37°53.81' W 107°42.78'

▼ 0.1   SO Mine remains.
▼ 1.0   BR Road forks. To the left is Southwest
            #23: Bullion King Lake Trail.
▼ 1.2   BR Track on left. Waterfall on right.
▼ 1.3   SO Track on right.
▼ 2.9   BL Road forks.
▼ 3.2   Summit of Black Bear Pass. Zero trip
            meter.
            GPS: N 37°53.99' W 107°44.52'

▼ 0.0   Proceed from the summit on main
            track, heading northwest down the hill.
▼ 1.6   SO Track on left to Ingram Lake.
▼ 1.8   SO Spectacular view of Telluride on left.
▼ 2.1   BL Track on right goes to Black Bear
            Mine. Cross through creek.
▼ 2.6   SO Very tight downhill switchback.
▼ 2.8   SO Mine portal on the right side of road.
▼ 3.2   SO Mine on left.
▼ 3.3   SO Cross through Ingram Creek at Ingram
            Falls. Mine ruins.
            GPS: N 37°55.34' W 107°45.60'

▼ 4.1   UT One-way sign. End of difficult section.
            Closed driveway to old power station
            on left.
▼ 4.7   SO Mine entrance (closed) on right.
▼ 5.0   SO Parking at Bridal Veil Falls.

SW Trail #22: Black Bear Pass Trail

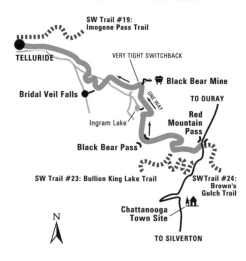

▼ 5.5   SO Cross Ingram Falls runoff.
▼ 5.8   SO Cross over creek.
▼ 6.4   SO Tracks on left and right.
▼ 6.5   BL Entrance to Pandora Mill on right (no
            access).
▼ 6.6   SO Tailing ponds on left and Pandora Mill
            on right.
            GPS: N 37°55.84' W 107°46.70'

▼ 6.9   SO Road changes from dirt to paved surface.
▼ 8.0   SO Telluride Cemetery on right.
▼ 8.4   SO Enter Telluride's main street (W. Colorado).
▼ 9.1   End at Visitor Information Center on W.
            Colorado (main street) in Telluride.
            GPS: N 37°56.37' W 107°49.15'

SOUTHWEST REGION TRAIL #23

Bullion King Lake Trail

STARTING POINT Southwest #22: Black Bear
Pass Trail
FINISHING POINT US 550
TOTAL MILEAGE 2.8 miles (one-way)
UNPAVED MILEAGE 2.8 miles
DRIVING TIME 1/2 hour
ROUTE ELEVATION 11,000 to 12,400 feet
USUALLY OPEN Mid-July to late September
DIFFICULTY RATING 3
SCENIC RATING 7

Special Attractions
- Attractive, panoramic scenery.
- Small alpine lakes.

Description
Most maps do not show this road, and those that do are not accurate.

This road can be used as a side route of Black Bear Pass Trail or as an alternative for those not wishing to tangle with Black Bear—one of the most notorious 4WD roads in the San Juans. It provides some wonderfully panoramic scenery and an opportunity for a short hike to a few small, tranquil alpine lakes at the end of the trail.

The route commences one mile along Southwest #22: Black Bear Pass Trail. It includes a section of narrow shelf road, a hundred feet or more above Porphyry Gulch Creek, which is sound but provides little opportunity for passing oncoming vehicles. It therefore pays to look ahead and let any oncoming vehicles come through before proceeding.

Taking a side road toward Silverton rather than returning all the way to Black Bear Pass Trail can vary the return trip.

Current Road Condition Information
Uncompahgre National Forest
Ouray Ranger District
2505 South Townsend Avenue
Montrose, CO 81401
(970) 240-5300

Map References
USFS San Juan NF
USGS San Juan County
Trails Illustrated, #141
Colorado Atlas & Gazetteer, p. 76

Route Directions

▼ 0.0   Begin at the intersection of US 550 and Southwest #22: Black Bear Pass Trail (FR 823), just south of the summit marker of Red Mountain. Only a small, brown 4WD signpost marks the track. Zero trip meter and proceed along FR 823.

2.8 ▲   End at intersection with US 550.
GPS: N 37°53.81′ W 107°42.78′

▼ 0.1   SO   Mine remains.
2.7 ▲   SO   Mine remains.

▼ 1.0   BL   Road forks. Black Bear Pass Trail continues on the right fork.
1.8 ▲   BR   Intersection with Southwest #22: Black Bear Pass Trail. Left goes to Black Bear Pass and right goes to US 550.
GPS: N 37°53.70′ W 107°43.51′

▼ 1.1   SO   Cross through creek.
1.7 ▲   SO   Cross through creek.

▼ 1.3   SO   Track on left to campsite. Then cross through creek.
1.5 ▲   SO   Cross through creek. Track on right to campsite.

▼ 1.4   SO   Track on left to campsite on cliff.
1.4 ▲   SO   Track on right to campsite on cliff.

▼ 1.5   BR   Track on left to campsite. Then alternate route from US 550 enters on left.
1.3 ▲   BL   Alternate route from US 550 enters on right.

▼ 2.3   SO   Mine remains on the left. Cross through creek. Mine remains on the right.
0.5 ▲   SO   Mine remains on the left. Cross through creek. Mine remains on the right.

▼ 2.6   SO   Cross through creek.
0.2 ▲   SO   Cross through creek.

▼ 2.7   SO   Waterfall on right.
0.1 ▲   SO   Waterfall on left.

▼ 2.8   Road comes to an end. Follow walking path to Bullion King Lake. Zero trip meter.
0.0 ▲   UT   Turn around and proceed back down the mountain away from Bullion King Lake.
GPS: N 37°53.16′ W 107°44.42′

SW Trail #23: Bullion King Lake Trail

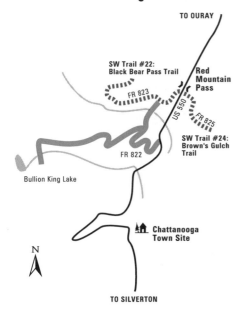

SW Trail #22: Black Bear Pass Trail
TO OURAY
Red Mountain Pass
FR 823
US 550
FR 825
SW Trail #24: Brown's Gulch Trail
FR 822
Bullion King Lake
Chattanooga Town Site
N
TO SILVERTON

▼ 0.0   UT   Turn around and proceed back down the mountain away from Bullion King Lake.

2.8 ▲   Road comes to an end. Follow walking path to Bullion King Lake. Zero trip meter.

▼ 0.1   SO   Waterfall on left.
2.7 ▲   SO   Waterfall on right.

▼ 0.2   SO   Cross through creek.
2.6 ▲   SO   Cross through creek.

▼ 0.5   SO   Mine remains on the left. Cross through creek. Mine remains on the right.
2.3 ▲   SO   Mine remains on the left. Cross through creek. Mine remains on the right.

▼ 1.3   BR   Fork in road. Left reconnects with Black Bear Pass Trail.
1.5 ▲   BL   Fork in road.

▼ 1.6   BR   Track on left.
1.2 ▲   BL   Track on right.

▼ 2.2   SO   Campsite on right.
0.6 ▲   SO   Campsite on left.

▼ 2.7   SO   Fork in road to private cabin.
0.1 ▲   BR   Fork in road to private cabin.

▼ 2.8   End at US 550.
0.0 ▲   At the intersection of US 550 and FR 822, zero trip meter and proceed west on FR 822.

GPS: N 37°53.33′ W 107°43.12′

Brown's Gulch Trail

STARTING POINT Intersection with US 550, 0.2 miles south of Red Mountain Pass

FINISHING POINT Intersection with US 550, 0.7 miles north of turnoff to Southwest #20: Ophir Pass Trail

TOTAL MILEAGE 5.8 miles

UNPAVED MILEAGE 5.8 miles

DRIVING TIME 1 hours

ROUTE ELEVATION 10,200 to 12,100 feet

USUALLY OPEN June to October

DIFFICULTY RATING 3

SCENIC RATING 8

Special Attractions

- Great views of the of U.S. Basin and the surrounding mountains.
- Historic mining area.
- Located near many other trails.

Description

The entrance to this trail is unmarked. It is located opposite the entrance to Southwest #22: Black Bear Pass Trail. There are some old buildings that were part of the Longfellow Mine on the left at the entrance to the trail. Although long since deserted, they are in good condition.

The trail climbs through the forest after leaving US 550. It is narrow but passing oncoming vehicles is not a problem. After about two miles, the trail rises above timberline and the view opens up. Initially,

A view of the trail near an overlook into U.S. Basin

there is a good view to the west with Red Mountain in the foreground and beyond it to the row of mountain peaks from Ophir Pass to Black Bear Pass. A short distance farther along, as you travel just below the ridgeline, a short walk provides a wonderful view down into U.S. Basin and across to McMillan Peak to the east.

Continuing, the trail descends to reenter the forest. The road travels through some recent mining operations before switchbacking down the mountain to rejoin US 550.

The road is reasonably steep in places and can become muddy. However, under good weather conditions the surface is sound and should not pose problems. There are only a few short sections of shelf road, all of which are low on the "white knuckle" rating.

Current Road Condition Information
San Juan National Forest
701 Camino del Rio
Durango, CO 81301
(970) 247-4874

Map References
USFS San Juan NF or Uncompahgre NF
USGS San Juan County
Trails Illustrated, #141
The Roads of Colorado, p. 115
Colorado Atlas & Gazetteer, p. 76

Route Directions

▼ 0.0   From the top of Red Mountain Pass on US 550, proceed east onto the unmarked track beside old buildings from the Longfellow Mine and zero trip meter. This turn is approximately opposite Southwest #22: Black Bear Pass Trail.

5.8 ▲   End at intersection with US 550 at Red Mountain Pass.
          GPS: N 37°53.76' W 107°42.79'

▼ 0.1 BR Track on left. Follow sign to US Basin (FR 825).
5.7 ▲ BL Track on right.

▼ 0.2 SO Track on right.
5.6 ▲ SO Track on left.

▼ 0.7 BR Track on left. Then cross over creek.
5.1 ▲ BL Cross over creek. Then track on right.

▼ 0.8 BL Fork in road. Track on right goes to private property.
5.0 ▲ SO Entrance to private property is on left.

▼ 0.9 SO Cross over creek.
4.9 ▲ SO Cross over creek.

▼ 1.0 BR Track on left.

SW Trail #24: Brown's Gulch Trail

4.8 ▲　BL　Track on right.

▼ 1.3　SO　Cross through creek.
4.5 ▲　SO　Cross through creek.

▼ 2.8　SO　Faint track on left to a scenic overlook of mountains and basin; a cabin is visible on mountain across the valley.
3.0 ▲　SO　Faint track on right to an overlook; a cabin is visible on mountain across the valley.
　　　　GPS: N 37°52.98′ W 107°42.33′

▼ 3.6　SO　Track on right.
2.2 ▲　SO　Track on left.

▼ 3.7　BL　Track on right. Then bear right at the fork in road.
2.1 ▲　BR　Continue past track entering on right. Then bear right at the next fork.

▼ 3.8　SO　Road enters on left. Pass through mining area.
1.9 ▲　BL　Mining operations area. Fork in road.

▼ 3.9　SO　Mine portal on left.
1.8 ▲　SO　Mine portal on right.

▼ 4.1　SO　Cross over creek.
1.7 ▲　SO　Cross over creek.

▼ 5.8　　　End at intersection with US 550.
0.0 ▲　　　From US 550 (about 0.7 miles north of Southwest #20: Ophir Pass Trail), zero trip meter and proceed east along FR 825-an unmarked dirt track.
　　　　GPS: N 37°51.50′ W 107°43.40′

Bandora Mine and Clear Lake Trail

STARTING POINT Intersection of US 550 and County 7/FR 585
FINISHING POINT Clear Lake
TOTAL MILEAGE 14.5 miles (to Clear Lake)
UNPAVED MILEAGE 14.5 miles
DRIVING TIME 1 hour
ROUTE ELEVATION 9,600 to 12,300 feet
USUALLY OPEN June to October
DIFFICULTY RATING 3
SCENIC RATING 9

Special Attractions
- Very scenic, particularly the picturesque setting of Clear Lake.
- Good camping, both developed and backcountry.

History
Silver was first discovered along Mineral Creek in 1882 and several rich strikes followed. The Bandora Mine was acquired by the Blanco Mining Company in 1940 and worked into the 1950s. By that time there were no accommodations for the miners at the mine and most traveled from Silverton.

A section of the trail as it switchbacks up to Clear Lake

Description

To start this trail you turn off US 550 onto County 7, a maintained gravel road, and proceed toward Mineral Creek Campground. The road travels beside South Mineral Creek, along which you can see numerous ponds and lodges created by ever-industrious beavers.

Clear Lake

The route directions first take you to Bandora Mine and then to Clear Lake. At the 3.7-mile point, you pass the turnoff for the lake on the right-hand side, which is worth noting because after traveling to the Bandora Mine and South Park, the route directions will bring you back to this point to go to Clear Lake.

Shortly after this intersection, you pass the USFS Mineral Creek Campground on the left. There are also many good back-country camping opportunities along this trail. After the campground, the road gets rougher but it is not difficult. You travel through a short section of dense forest and then through open scrub country before passing below Bandora Mine and entering a large, level meadow known as South Park. This segment of the route finishes at an old cabin on the far side of the park.

Return to the turnoff to Clear Lake that you passed earlier, zero your trip meter and turn left, proceeding toward Clear Lake. You immediately start to ascend as you travel through the pine and spruce forest. Although this part of the route is along a shelf, it is not difficult and there are plenty of passing spots. It is a little rough and rocky, but the surface is sound.

The road continues to switchback up the mountain, rising above timberline and providing a couple of good observation points for the waterfalls created by Clear Creek. Finally, the road levels off as you enter the very picturesque basin that cradles Clear Lake.

Current Road Condition Information
San Juan National Forest
701 Camino del Rio
Durango, CO 81301
(970) 247-4874

Map References
USFS San Juan NF or Uncompahgre NF
USGS San Juan County
Trails Illustrated, #141
The Roads of Colorado, pp. 114–115
Colorado Atlas & Gazetteer, p. 76

Route Directions

▼ 0.0   From US 550, zero trip meter and turn onto County 7/FR 585. A sign indicates this is a NF Access road to South Mineral Campground.
GPS: N 37°49.11' W 107°42.10'

▼ 1.0   SO Cross over bridge.
▼ 1.6   SO Track on right.
▼ 2.3   SO Cross over creek.
▼ 3.7   BL Fork in road. Turning right goes to Clear Lake (you will return to this intersection later). Continue toward USFS Mineral Campground, remaining on main road.
GPS: N 37°48.32' W 107°45.74'

▼ 4.3   SO USFS South Mineral Campground on left. Parking on right. Continue straight ahead.
GPS: N 37°48.29' W 107°46.31'

▼ 4.5   SO Cross over creek with Rico-Silverton Trailhead and waterfall on the right.
▼ 6.3   SO Cross through creek.
▼ 6.4   SO Bandora Mine and Mill ruins on the right.
GPS: N 37°47.20' W 107°47.99'

▼ 6.6   SO Track on left goes to a cabin.
▼ 6.7   SO Cross though creek.
▼ 6.9   End of track. A mining cabin is across the creek.
GPS: N 37°46.80' W 107°48.11'

SW Trail #25: Bandora Mine and Clear Lake Trail

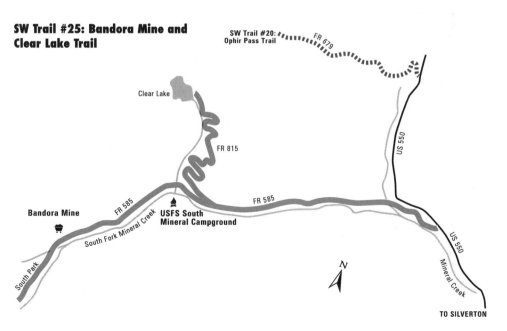

Continuation from Clear Lake turnoff

▼ 0.0　From County 7 (South Mineral Creek Campground access road), zero trip meter and proceed up the hill.
　　　　N 37°48.32' W 107°45.74'

▼ 2.8　SO　Closure gate.
▼ 3.3　SO　Waterfall on left.
　　　　N 37°49.22' W 107°46.46'

▼ 3.5　SO　Mine straight ahead at switchback. Proceed up hill.
　　　　N 37°49.17' W 107°46.33'

▼ 4.1　BR　Track on left goes on up the mountain.
▼ 4.4　End of trail at beautiful Clear Lake.
　　　　N 37°49.58' W 107°46.90'

SOUTHWEST REGION TRAIL #26

Cunningham Gulch and Stony Pass Trail

STARTING POINT Howardsville from Southwest #6: Silverton to Animas Forks Ghost Town road
FINISHING POINT Intersection of FR 520 and Colorado 149, between Lake City and Creede
TOTAL MILEAGE 37.7 miles
UNPAVED MILEAGE 37.2 miles
DRIVING TIME 3 1/4 hours
ROUTE ELEVATION 9,200 to 12,588 feet
USUALLY OPEN Mid-June to late October
DIFFICULTY RATING 5
SCENIC RATING 9

Special Attractions

■ A varied and scenic 4WD trail.
■ A challenging stream crossing.
■ Relative solitude; this trail has less traffic than many others in the peak summer months.

History

Cunningham Gulch is named for Major W. H. Cunningham, who brought a party of mining investors from Chicago through the area. Stony Pass got its name because of its rocky terrain. It was also known as Hamilton Pass, after the builder of the first wagon road over the pass, and as Rio Grande Pass.

The Stony Pass crossing holds a great deal of historic interest. The Ute used the trail for centuries, and Spanish artifacts have also been found in the area. The pass is believed to have been discovered in 1860 by Charles Baker, who led a party of prospectors to the area, well before the Brunot Treaty officially opened the territory in 1873.

Major E. M. Hamilton built a wagon road along the route in 1872, which was improved seven years later. During this period, the road was heavily used as a stage route and a major supply line for the four thousand mines operating in the area.

When the railroad reached Silverton in 1882, the pass was used less often. However, the route remained open and was at one point early this century was classified as a state highway. Eventually, it was completely abandoned until the Forest Service reopened it in the 1950s as a 4WD recreational route.

This route starts in the town of Howardsville, originally named Bullion City for the Bullion City Company, which laid out the town as a promotional settlement in late 1872. However, the following year the residents changed the name to Howardsville, after the individual who built the first cabin on the site.

Because Howardsville was growing at the same time as nearby Silverton, the two towns became rivals. Howardsville was named the first county seat in Colorado in 1874, but the following year voters moved the county seat to Silverton. Howardsville consisted of about thirty buildings and at its peak had about 150 residents. The post office that served Howardsville was claimed to have been the first one in western Colorado; it was in operation from 1874 to 1939.

Highland Mary, a town near the Highland Mary Mill and Highland Mary Mine at the top of Cunningham Gulch, was founded by two brothers from New York

Cunningham Gulch

who decided to head west to seek their fortune in silver. The enterprising Ennis brothers took the rather eccentric step of consulting a fortune-teller to decide where they should begin prospecting. The fortune-teller reportedly pointed to an area on the map where the two would find treasure.

The brothers named the area the Highland Mary and continued to visit the spiritualist for advice. Her instructions regarding where and how to find ore led the brothers on a peculiar search through the mountains, during which they unknowingly crossed over some rich gold veins. Occasionally they made some lucky discoveries. By 1885, the Ennises had invested about a million dollars in the mine and had paid the spiritualist another fifty thousand. The pair ended up bankrupt; they sold the mine and their nearby elaborate house and returned to New York.

The new owners of the mine prospected by more conventional methods, and Highland Mary immediately began to pay off. It became one of the best mines in Cunningham Gulch and operated sporadically through the years until 1952. All that remains today are the ruins of the mill.

On the eastern side of the pass, near where Pole Creek flows into the Rio Grande River, is the site that was proposed for Junction City. The town was platted after ore was found in 1894, but the ore soon ran out and most of the miners left before any construction occurred.

Description

The route is a long 4WD trail with varied scenery. It sees light use compared to other, better known routes in the San Juans during summer. It is usually open by the middle of June.

The road starts at Howardsville, between Silverton and Animas Forks, as an attractive 2WD road, running alongside Cunningham Creek up Cunningham Gulch. Within a couple of miles it becomes steeper, narrower, and rougher as it climbs up a ledge overlooking the gulch. It soon narrows to the width of one vehicle with occasional pulloffs for passing.

As the road approaches the summit of

One lonely miner's cabin and some of the many mines near the summit of Stony Pass

Stony Pass, it levels out into a beautiful alpine valley with typical vegetation and many wildflowers. The open portals of mines and decaying cabins are still in evidence.

From the pass, the road tracks the edge of the Weminuche Wilderness Area and follows the headwaters of the Rio Grande River. At around the ten-mile point, the road offers great access to some scenic and quiet fishing spots.

The road from the summit has a relatively gentle grade. The biggest potential problems in the first ten miles of the descent are mud and occasional shallow creek crossings. The few rough stretches are relatively short.

At the 11.8-mile point is the Pole Creek crossing, which is the deepest of all the stream crossings covered in this book. If you are traveling early in the season, we advise you to start this trail in the morning because snowmelt causes the creek to rise significantly throughout the day. Later in the day, this crossing could be impassable or cause vehicle damage. Later in the season, the creek can still be two feet deep, but the bottom is sound. With good tires and a slow, steady pace, 4WD vehicles should have no problem crossing.

The degree of difficulty of the next few miles is a matter of how long it has been since the last rain. When wet, the road can be very muddy. Assess the situation and proceed cautiously when crossing the creeks; sharp approach and departure angles at these crossings can hang up your vehicle. The trail winds through forest in this section, so once it gets muddy, it can stay that way for some time. Clearance between the trees is narrow at times, and the road even has a couple of short, rocky sections.

Current Road Condition Information

San Juan National Forest
701 Camino del Rio
Durango, CO 81301
(970) 247-4874

Map References

USFS Uncompahgre NF
      Rio Grande NF
USGS San Juan County
      Hinsdale County #2
      Mineral County #1
Trails Illustrated, #140, #141
The Roads of Colorado, pp. 131–132
Colorado Atlas & Gazetteer, pp. 77–78

Route Directions

▼ 0.0   At intersection of Southwest #6 and the turnoff to Cunningham Gulch in Howardsville, zero trip meter and proceed toward Cunningham Gulch and Stony Pass.

5.8 ▲   End at intersection with Southwest #6: Silverton to Animas Forks Ghost Town.

GPS: N 37°50.12' W 107°35.69'

▼ 0.2   BR   Fork in road. Left goes to Old Hundred Mine.

5.6 ▲   SO   Road on right to Old Hundred Mine.

▼ 1.0   SO   Old Hundred Mine and Mill on left.

4.8 ▲   SO   Old Hundred Mine and Mill on right.

▼ 1.3   SO   Site of Green Mountain Mill on right.

4.5 ▲   SO   Site of Green Mountain Mill on left.

▼ 1.5   SO   Buffalo Boy Tramhouse and Tramway on left.

4.3 ▲   SO   Buffalo Boy Tramhouse and Tramway on right.

▼ 1.7   BR/BL   Follow sign to Creede via Stony Pass on County 3. Road enters on left and goes back to Old Hundred Mine. Then road forks and the track on right goes to the town site of Highland Mary in 3.4 miles.

4.1 ▲   BL/BR   Intersection. Roads enter on left and right. Continue on middle road.

▼ 2.5   SO   Cross through creek.

3.3 ▲   SO   Cross through creek.

▼ 3.2   BR   Short track on left.

2.6 ▲   BL   Short track on right.

▼ 3.3   BR   Track on left.

2.5 ▲   BL   Track on right.

▼ 3.5   BL   Cross under tramway. Track entering on right.

2.3 ▲   BR   Track entering on left. Cross under tramway.

▼ 3.7   SO   Small bridge over creek.

2.1   SO   Small bridge over creek.

▼ 4.0   SO   Cross over creek. Small track on right.

1.8 ▲   SO   Small track on left. Cross over creek.

▼ 4.7   SO   Small track on right.

1.1 ▲   SO   Small track on left.

▼ 5.8   SO   Summit of Stony Pass. Zero trip meter.

0.0 ▲   Continue along road.

GPS: N 37°47.75' W 107°32.93'

▼ 0.0   Continue along road.

6.2 ▲   SO   Summit of Stony Pass. Zero trip meter.

▼ 0.2   SO   Cabin and mine tracks on right.

6.0 ▲   SO   Cabin and mine tracks on left.

▼ 1.0   SO   West Ute Creek and Ute Creek trails.

5.2 ▲   SO   West Ute Creek and Ute Creek trails.

▼ 1.3   SO   Cross over creek.

4.9 ▲   SO   Cross over creek.

▼ 3.6   SO   Cross over creek.

2.6 ▲   SO   Cross over creek.

▼ 5.3   SO   Track to river on right.

0.9 ▲   SO   Track to river on left.

▼ 5.4   SO   Pass through fence line.

0.8 ▲   SO   Pass through fence line.

▼ 6.0   SO   Cross through Pole Creek. Beware that this crossing may be deep.

0.2 ▲   SO   Cross through Pole Creek. Beware that this crossing may be deep.

GPS: N 37°45.86' W 107°28.00'

▼ 6.2   BL   Intersection. FR 506 on right goes to Beartown site and Kite Lake. Town site of Junction City. Zero trip meter.

0.0 ▲   Continue toward Stony Pass and Silverton.

GPS: N 37°45.72' W 107°27.97'

▼ 0.0   Continue toward Rio Grande Reservoir and Creede. Pole Creek Trail is on left.

16.2 ▲   SO   Pole Creek Trail on right. Intersection. FR 506 on left goes to Beartown site

SW Trail #26: Cunningham Gulch and Stony Pass Trail

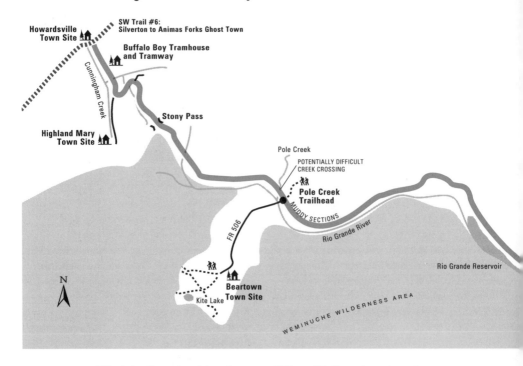

and Kite Lake. Town site of Junction City. Zero trip meter.

▼ 0.7   SO Cross through creek.
15.5 ▲ SO Cross through creek.

▼ 1.0   SO Gate.
15.2 ▲ SO Gate.

▼ 2.1   SO Cross through Sweetwater Creek.
14.1 ▲ SO Cross through Sweetwater Creek.

▼ 2.3-2.5 SO Beaver ponds and dams on right.
13.7-13.9 ▲SO Beaver ponds and dams on left.

▼ 2.9   SO Cross through creek.
13.3 ▲ SO Cross through creek.

▼ 3.0   SO Water crossing. This one can be deep.
13.2 ▲ SO Water crossing. This one can be deep.

▼ 3.2   SO Cross through creek.
13.0 ▲ SO Cross through creek.

▼ 3.5   SO Cross through creek.

12.7 ▲ SO Cross through creek.

▼ 4.3   SO Cross through creek.
11.9 ▲ SO Cross through creek.

▼ 4.4-4.8 SO Series of water crossings. None difficult.
11.4-11.8▲SO Series of water crossings. None difficult.

▼ 5.0   SO Cattle guard. Cross through creek.
11.2 ▲ SO Cross through creek. Cattle guard. Sign reads "Brewster Park."

▼ 5.7   SO Track on right to river.
10.5 ▲ SO Track on left to river.

▼ 6.5   BR Track on left. Cross through creek.
9.7 ▲ SO Cross through creek. Track on right.

▼ 6.7   SO Track to campsites on right.
9.5 ▲ SO Track to campsites on left.

▼ 7.1   SO Track on right.
9.1 ▲ SO Track on left.

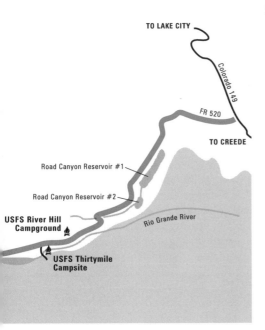

TO LAKE CITY

Colorado 149

FR 520

TO CREEDE

Road Canyon Reservoir #1

Road Canyon Reservoir #2

Rio Grande River

USFS River Hill Campground

USFS Thirtymile Campsite

▼ 7.9   SO Lost Trail Creek Trailhead on left. Cattle guard.

8.3 ▲   SO Cattle guard. Lost Trail Creek Trailhead on right.

▼ 8.3   SO Bridge over creek. Lost Trail Campground on right.

7.9 ▲   SO Lost Trail Campground on left. Bridge over creek.

▼ 9.1   SO Ute Creek Trailhead on right. Public restrooms.

7.1 ▲   SO Public restrooms. Ute Creek Trailhead on left.

▼ 10.1   SO Cattle guard. Overlook to Rio Grande Reservoir.

6.1 ▲   SO Overlook to Rio Grande Reservoir. Cattle guard.

GPS: N 37°44.99′ W 107°19.87′

▼ 13.2   SO Track on right to reservoir. Public restrooms available.

3.0 ▲   SO Track on left to reservoir. Public restrooms available.

▼ 14.2   SO Seasonal closure gate. Track on right to Rio Grande Reservoir (no access).

2.0 ▲   SO Track on left to Rio Grande Reservoir (no access). Seasonal closure gate.

GPS: N 37°43.35′ W 107°16.00′

▼ 14.8   SO Turnoff on right to USFS Thirtymile Campground, Weminuche Trailhead, Thirtymile Resort, and Squaw Creek Trailhead.

1.4 ▲   SO Turnoff on left to USFS Thirtymile Campground, Weminuche Trailhead, Thirtymile Resort, and Squaw Creek Trailhead.

▼ 16.2   SO USFS River Hill Campground. Zero trip meter.

0.0 ▲   Continue along main road toward Stony Pass.

GPS: N 37°43.81′ W 107°13.86′

▼ 0.0   Continue along main road.

9.5 ▲   SO USFS River Hill Campground. Zero trip meter.

▼ 1.2   SO Cattle guard. Road on left to Sawmill Canyon.

8.3 ▲   SO Road on right to Sawmill Canyon. Cattle guard.

▼ 2.8-4.8 SO Road Canyon Reservoirs #1 and #2 on right.

4.7-6.7 ▲SO Road Canyon Reservoirs #1 and #2 on left.

▼ 3.3   SO USFS campground.

6.2 ▲   SO USFS campground.

▼ 3.6   SO Seasonal gate.

5.9 ▲   SO Seasonal gate.

▼ 4.4   SO Public toilets.

5.1 ▲   SO Public toilets.

▼ 5.1   SO Public toilets.

4.4 ▲   SO Public toilets.

▼ 6.2   BR Fork in the road.

3.3 ▲   BL Track on right.

▼ 6.8	SO	Cattle guard.
2.7 ▲	SO	Cattle guard

▼ 9.0	SO	Pavement begins.
0.5 ▲	SO	Unpaved road.

▼ 9.5		Cattle guard. Stop sign. End at inter-section with Colorado 149. Lake City is approximately 32 miles to the left; Creede is approximately 20 miles to the right.
0.0 ▲		At intersection of Colorado 149 with FR 520, zero trip meter and proceed onto FR 520. Creede is approximately 20 miles east.

GPS: N 37°47.41′ W 107°07.71′

SOUTHWEST REGION TRAIL #27

Summitville Ghost Town Trail

STARTING POINT Intersection of Colorado 17 and FR 250

FINISHING POINT Del Norte

TOTAL MILEAGE 68.3 miles

UNPAVED MILEAGE 57.9 miles

DRIVING TIME 4 hours

ROUTE ELEVATION 8,000 to 11,900 feet

USUALLY OPEN Early July to late October

DIFFICULTY RATING 2

SCENIC RATING 6

Special Attractions

- The well-preserved ghost town of Summitville.
- An easy 4WD trail that is not heavily used.

History

This route crosses Stunner Pass and skirts Elwood Pass, both of which were part of two early access roads through the area. The first road over Stunner Pass was constructed in 1884 by the LeDuc and Sanchez Toll Road Company as a freight route to service mines

that had started activity in the early 1880s. Mining activity was short-lived, and by the early 1890s, the area was almost deserted. However, the route has been maintained for recreational access to the area.

The U.S. army constructed a road across Elwood Pass in 1878 to connect Fort Garland and Fort Harris in Pagosa Springs. In the 1880s, mining began in the area, and significant deposits of gold and silver were found. Summitville ghost town is the best-preserved of the mining camps from this period; numerous buildings still stand.

Gold was discovered in the Summitville area in 1870, and hundreds of prospectors descended on the area. At its peak, the town had a population of more than 600 and 2,500 mining claims were staked. It boomed during the 1880s and produced a fortune for Tom Bowen, who became a leading figure in Colorado politics and a great rival of Horace Tabor. The town was in decline by 1890 and deserted by 1893.

Shortly, before the halfway point of the trail you pass the township of Platoro, which was established after ore was discovered in 1882. It was named for the Spanish words plata and oro meaning silver and gold. Because of its inaccessibility, ore and supplies could be transported only by burro. In 1888, the wagon road to Summitville was completed and the town grew to a population of 300 by 1890. However, the ore in the area was of indifferent quality and the miners drifted away.

Although little is known about the township of Stunner, located a short distance northwest of Platoro, it is suspected that the first construction occurred in 1882. Both gold and silver were mined in the vicinity, but the remoteness of the camp prevented proper development. No railroad came through Stunner, but the LeDuc and Sanchez Toll Road Company built a road to the area.

Between 100 and 150 people lived in Stunner in its best days. A post office was established in 1890, but the town lasted only a few more years. Stunner's decline began because of the high costs of transporting ore from the area's mines and was speeded by the

A section of the trail beside Conejos River near Platoro

lack of good ores to justify these costs. Because nearby Summitville (on the other side of the range) offered better ore and lower transportation costs, Stunner's population began to dwindle. There is nothing left of Stunner. A U.S. Forest Service ranger station and the Stunner Campground are on the site of the old town.

Summitville, on South Mountain, at 11,200 feet, was once the highest of Colorado's major gold camps. In 1870, miner John Esmund discovered rich ore in abundance near the area that years later would become the Summitville mining camp. After Esmund's initial discovery, he returned to the location several times to extract ore, during which time he failed to file proper paperwork to make the claim legally his. When he showed up at the site in 1873, he found that someone else had established a mine on his spot. The

mine, the Little Annie, became the best gold-producing mine in the area.

By 1882, Summitville had swelled to a population of more than 1,500; there were several hotels, the *Summitville Nugget* newspaper, saloons, stores, and nine mills at which to process the ore. One of the mining

Stunner in 1913

companies set up a pool hall to entertain the men during their free time, especially over the long winter months. The hall attracted pool sharks from all over the state who came to match skills with the miners.

Del Norte, about twenty-four miles northeast of Summitville, was an important shipping point, supply center, and stagecoach junction. One of its residents, Tom Bowen, struck it rich with his Little Ida Mine in Summitville. Suave and colorful, Bowen wore many hats; and his skill and luck were legendary. Over the course of his life, Bowen was a judge, an entrepreneur, a lawyer, the governor of Idaho Territory, brigadier general for the Union army, a U.S. senator, and a very big gambler. Bowen once lost shares of a mining company in a poker game, only to have the winner decide he didn't want the shares. Bowen redeemed the stock for a nominal purchase; and the mine, the Little Ida, later made him very rich. He purchased many other mining properties, including the Little Annie.

In 1885, some of the mines in the area began having financial difficulties and even

MINING OPERATIONS

Gold and silver deposits are frequently found together. Both are formed when molten minerals are forced up from deep within the earth into the bedrock. Usually gold and silver also exist with other minerals such as pyrite (fool's gold) and galena (which has a silvery appearance). Commonly, the host rock is quartz.

Over time, erosion breaks down the rock deposits and the gold is freed and left in pure form. Water then disperses the free gold along streambeds. In its free form, gold exists in a variety of shapes: nuggets, scale, shot, grains, dust. These free deposits are known as "placers" when the gold is found in streambeds or along stream banks. A deposit of gold that is contained in a rock formation is called a "lode."

Placer Mining. Because placers are relatively easy to find, they are normally the first gold deposits discovered in any area. Miners typically follow the placers upstream to the mother lode.

Placer mining is the simplest form of mining operations, because it merely involves separating the free gold from the dirt, mud, or gravel with which it is mixed. The process takes a number of forms:

- simple panning
- sluicing to process a larger volume, using the same principle as panning
- dredging to process even larger volumes of rock (Dredge mining utilizes a power-driven chain of small buckets mounted on a barge, leaving in its wake squalid piles of washed rock to mark its course for decades to come. Processing tons of rock and soil quickly, dredges overcame the problem of large quantities of low-grade gravel. Dredges could move up to three-quarters of a million yards of earth per annum.)
- hydraulic mining (used where the ancient riverbeds had long since disappeared, leaving the gold on dry land and some distance from any existing stream. Hydraulic mining uses hoses to bring water from up to three miles distant and wash away the extraneous material to recover the gold.)

Placer mining was known as "poor man's mining" because panning a creek could be done with very little capital. Colorado's placer production has been nearly all gold.

Hard-Rock Mining. Hard-rock mining involves digging ore out of the ground and recovering it from the quartz (or other minerals) surrounding it. Hard-rock mining in its simplest form involves tunneling horizontally under the vein (either directly or from an initial vertical shaft), then digging out the ore into mine cars placed beneath it. In the 1800s, mining cars were pulled by mules along tracks laid in the mines. If

the Little Annie could not pay workers' salaries. Other mines were playing out, so the population of Summitville rapidly declined. By 1889, only about twenty-five residents remained in town.

There were a few short revivals in mining: one in the late 1890s and another in the late 1930s. In recent years, Galactic Resources, Ltd. re-opened operations, but they suffered heavy losses through 1991 and sold the balance of their mining interests. In 1993, Galactic filed for bankruptcy.

Although some of the ghost town's buildings have been torn down to make room for modern-day mining, a number of well-preserved buildings still stand in Summitville. It is an interesting ghost town to explore and photograph.

Description

The first section of this route via FR 250 over Stunner Pass is a well-maintained dirt road. The pass stretches between the Alamosa River to the north and the Conejos River to the south.

It offers a peaceful journey through gentle,

the mine incorporated a vertical shaft, then a hoist would lift the ore to the surface. Digging the shafts was made much easier during the 1870s, when hand drilling techniques were made obsolete by machine drills and dynamite.

Once extracted from the mine, the gold had to be separated from the host rock. To do this economically in the latter half of the nineteenth century, mining companies made use of stamp mills. Large structures that processed the ore in stages, stamp mills required water and a downhill slope. Milling involved progressively crushing the ore, then processing it chemically to extract the precious metal. Mine workers brought the ore into the mill and fed it into a stamper, which weighed up to a ton. The stamper crushed the host rock; then a slurry of the crushed ore and water was fed over a series of mercury-coated amalgamation plates, which captured the precious metal.

Because hard-rock mining required substantial capital, only large mining corporations normally undertook hard-rock mining operations. The men who worked the mines were employees of the larger corporations.

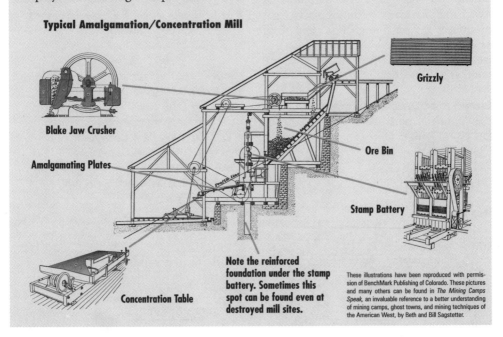

Typical Amalgamation/Concentration Mill

Blake Jaw Crusher

Amalgamating Plates

Concentration Table

Note the reinforced foundation under the stamp battery. Sometimes this spot can be found even at destroyed mill sites.

Grizzly

Ore Bin

Stamp Battery

These illustrations have been reproduced with permission of BenchMark Publishing of Colorado. These pictures and many others can be found in *The Mining Camps Speak,* an invaluable reference to a better understanding of mining camps, ghost towns, and mining techniques of the American West, by Beth and Bill Sagstetter.

Miner's boardinghouse at Summitville ghost town

rolling hills, interspersed with rock formations and overlooks that provide wonderful views along the valley and across the mountains. Abundant aspen groves spangle the hillsides in gold during the fall. The area also offers many accessible campsites and hiking trails.

In good weather conditions, the Stunner Pass section (FR 250) of this route warrants a difficulty rating of only 1. The Elwood Pass section (FR 380) is more difficult and causes this route to be rated at 2; although FR 380 is higher, narrower, and rougher than FR 250, it is a relatively easy route and should provide no obstacles for a 4WD vehicle.

The area offers an extensive network of 4WD and hiking trails. Mining activity has continued in the Summitville area until recent times, although presently operations are restricted to an EPA-mandated clean-up of the mine remains.

Current Road Condition Information
Rio Grande National Forest
Del Norte Ranger District
13308 West Hwy 160
Del Norte, CO 81132
(719) 657-3321

Map References
USFS Rio Grande NF
USGS Conejos County #1
        Rio Grande County #1
        Rio Grande County #2
Trails Illustrated, #142
The Roads of Colorado, pp. 133–134, 149–150
Colorado Atlas & Gazetteer, pp. 79, 89

Route Directions

▼ 0.0   At intersection of Colorado 17 and FR 250, zero trip meter. There is a signpost for Platoro. Turn onto the unpaved road.
16.1 ▲   End at intersection of Colorado 17 and FR 250.
         GPS: N 37°07.98' W 106°21.01'

▼ 6.0   SO Cattle guard. USFS Spectacle Lake Campground.
10.1 ▲   SO USFS Spectacle Lake Campground. Cattle guard.

▼ 6.3   SO USFS Conejos Campground.
9.8 ▲   SO USFS Conejos Campground.

▼ 7.4   SO Intersection. FR 855 on left goes to Rybold Lake and No Name Lake.
8.7 ▲   SO Intersection. FR 855 on right goes to Rybold Lake and No Name Lake.

▼ 8.8   SO Cattle guard.
7.3 ▲   SO Cattle guard.

▼ 10.8   SO Southfork Trailhead.
5.3 ▲   SO Southfork Trailhead.

▼ 11.1   SO Intersection. Track on left for fishing access. Public restrooms.
5.0 ▲   SO Intersection. Track on right for fishing access. Public restrooms.

▼ 11.8   SO Cattle guard.
4.3 ▲   SO Cattle guard.

▼ 13.2   SO Valdez Creek Campground.
2.9 ▲   SO Valdez Creek Campground.

▼ 13.8   SO Trail Creek backcountry camping area.
2.3 ▲   SO Trail Creek backcountry camping area.

▼ 13.9   SO Track on right.
2.2 ▲   SO Track on left.

▼ 14.2   SO Cattle guard.
1.9 ▲   SO Cattle guard.

▼ 16.1   SO Track on left is FR 100 to Lake Fork
         Ranch. Zero trip meter.
0.0 ▲   Proceed along main road.
         GPS: N 37°17.87′ W 106°28.63′

▼ 0.0   Proceed along main road.
12.0 ▲   SO Track on right is FR 100 to Lake Fork
         Ranch. Zero trip meter.

▼ 0.6   SO Cattle guard.
11.4 ▲   SO Cattle guard.

▼ 0.8   SO USFS Lake Fork Campground.
11.2 ▲   SO USFS Lake Fork Campground.

▼ 1.6   SO Beaver Lake Trailhead.
10.4 ▲   SO Beaver Lake Trailhead.

▼ 3.5   SO Fisher Gulch.
8.5 ▲   SO Fisher Gulch.

▼ 4.1   SO Track on right is FR 260 to Robinson
         Gulch.
7.9 ▲   SO Track on left is FR 260 to Robinson
         Gulch.

▼ 4.7   SO Cattle guard.
7.3 ▲   SO Cattle guard.

▼ 6.1   SO Intersection. Platoro on left.
5.9 ▲   SO Intersection. Platoro on right.
         GPS: N 37°21.25′ W 106°31.72′

▼ 6.5   SO Track on left to Mix Lake Campground.
5.5 ▲   SO Track on right to Mix Lake
         Campground.

▼ 7.6   TR T-intersection. Left goes to Mix Lake
         and Platoro Reservoir.
4.4 ▲   TL Intersection.

▼ 8.6   BL Stunner Pass (unmarked). FR 257
         on right goes to Lilly Pond and Kerr
         Lake.
3.4 ▲   BR FR 257 on left goes to Lilly Pond
         and Kerr Lake. Stunner Pass
         (unmarked).
         GPS: N 37°21.73′ W 106°33.44′

SW Trail #27: Summitville Ghost Town Trail

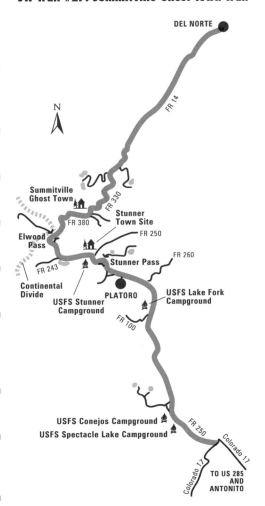

▼ 11.7   SO Bridge over Alamosa River. Campsites.
0.3 ▲   SO Campsites. Bridge over Alamosa River.

▼ 12.0   UT Intersection. Straight goes to Monte
         Vista. Zero trip meter.
0.0 ▲   Continue on FR 380.
         GPS: N 37°23.04′ W 106°33.95′

▼ 0.0   Continue on FR 380.
11.7 ▲   UT Intersection. Straight on goes to Monte
         Vista. Zero trip meter.

▼ 0.3   SO USFS Stunner Campground on left. Old
         cabin on right is part of Stunner town site.
11.4 ▲   SO Old cabin on left is part of Stunner

town site. USFS Stunner Campground on right.
GPS: N 37°22.88' W 106°34.21'

▼ 0.9   SO   Cattle guard.
10.8 ▲   SO   Cattle guard.

▼ 1.1   SO   Drainage ford.
10.6 ▲   SO   Drainage ford.

▼ 2.1   SO   Track on right.
9.6 ▲   SO   Track on left.

▼ 2.4   SO   Track on right.
9.3 ▲   SO   Track on left.

▼ 4.0   SO   Lake DeNelda on left (private property).
7.7 ▲   SO   Lake DeNelda on right (private property).

▼ 4.1   BR   Intersection. Dolores Canyon Road, Treasure Creek Road, and Lake Annella are straight ahead. Turn toward Summitville and US 160.
7.6 ▲   TL   Intersection. Dolores Canyon Road and Treasure Creek Road are to the right. Proceed toward Platoro.

▼ 4.6   SO   Cattle guard.
7.1 ▲   SO   Cattle guard.

▼ 6.5   SO   Track on right.
5.2 ▲   SO   Track on left.

▼ 7.7   SO   Crater Lake hiking trail on left.
4.0 ▲   SO   Crater Lake hiking trail on right.

▼ 8.4   SO   Intersection. Track and Continental Divide Trail on left. Elwood Pass is a short distance along it. Straight ahead is South Fork sign.
3.3 ▲   SO   Intersection. Track and Continental Divide Trail on right. Elwood Pass is a short distance along it.

▼ 8.7   SO   Elwood Cabin on right. Track FR 3802A on left.
3.0 ▲   SO   Elwood Cabin on left. Track FR 3802A on right.

▼ 9.6   SO   Track on right.

2.1 ▲   SO   Track on left.

▼ 9.8   SO   Cattle guard.
1.9 ▲   SO   Cattle guard.

▼ 11.7   TR   Intersection. Summitville ghost town to the right. Southfork to the left. Zero trip meter.
0.0 ▲   Proceed toward Platoro.
GPS: N 37°25.75' W 106°37.70'

▼ 0.0   Proceed toward Summitville.
2.5 ▲   TL   Intersection. Southfork to the right. Platoro to the left. Zero trip meter.

▼ 2.0   SO   Summitville Historic Mining Town sign.
0.5 ▲   SO   Summitville Historic Mining Town sign.

▼ 2.5   BL   Summitville visitor information board. Zero trip meter.
0.0 ▲   Continue on route.
GPS: N 37°25.93' W 106°35.94'

▼ 0.0   Continue on route.
26.5 ▲   BR   Summitville visitor information board. Zero trip meter.

▼ 0.1   TL   Turn onto FR 330.
26.4 ▲   TR   Intersection with FR 244.

▼ 0.3   SO   Intersection. Go toward Del Norte. Wightman Fork is to the right and forks off from the mining entrance.
26.2 ▲   SO   Intersection.

▼ 0.6   SO   Track on right.
25.9 ▲   SO   Track on left.

▼ 1.7   SO   Track on left.
24.8 ▲   SO   Track on right.

▼ 2.7   SO   Track on left.
23.8 ▲   SO   Track on right.

▼ 7.8   TR   Intersection. Crystal Lakes and South Fork to the left. Follow toward Del Norte.
18.7 ▲   BL   Intersection. Crystal Lakes and South Fork to the right.
GPS: N 37°29.31' W 106°32.81'

▼ 9.3 TL Cattle guard. Intersection. Fuches Reservoir and Blowout Pass to the right. Follow road to Del Norte (FR 14).

17.2 ▲ TR Intersection. Fuches Reservoir and Blowout Pass straight on. Follow FR 330. Cattle guard.

▼ 11.0 SO Road on left.
15.5 ▲ SO Road on right.

▼ 11.2 SO Cattle guard.
15.3 ▲ SO Cattle guard.

▼ 12.3 SO Track on right to campsite.
14.2 ▲ SO Track on left to campsite.

▼ 13.0 SO Track on left is FR 331 to Bear Creek.
13.5 ▲ SO Track on right is FR 331 to Bear Creek.

▼ 14.0 SO Track on right.
12.5 ▲ SO Track on left.

▼ 14.3 SO Track on right.
12.2 ▲ SO Track on left.

▼ 14.4 SO Track on right.
12.1 ▲ SO Track on left.

▼ 15.1 SO Seasonal gate.
11.4 ▲ SO Seasonal gate.

▼ 15.2 SO Cattle guard.
11.3 ▲ SO Cattle guard.

▼ 15.6 SO Pavement begins. Bridge.
10.9 ▲ SO Bridge. Unpaved.

▼ 24.4 SO Road 14A forks off on left.
2.1 ▲ SO Road 14A on right.

▼ 26.5 End at intersection of FR 14 and US 160 in Del Norte.

0.0 ▲ At intersection of FR 14 and US 160 in Del Norte, zero trip meter and proceed along FR 14. Sign reads "National Forest Access, Pinos Creek Rd, Summitville."

GPS: N 37°40.75′ W 106°21.66′

The last cabin remaining at the Graysill Mine site

Bolam Pass Trail

STARTING POINT Silverton
FINISHING POINT Intersection of FR 578 and Colorado 145
TOTAL MILEAGE 45.7 miles
UNPAVED MILEAGE 24.3 miles
DRIVING TIME 2 1/2 hours
ROUTE ELEVATION 9,200 to 11,340 feet
USUALLY OPEN Early July to October
DIFFICULTY RATING 2
SCENIC RATING 7

Special Attractions

- Attractive stream valley through the Purgatory ski area.
- Historic mining area of special significance in the effort to develop the first atomic bomb during World War II.
- Can connect with Southwest #29: Fall Creek Trail.

History

The Ute used Bolam Pass long before miners entered the area in the early 1860s. In 1881, the pass was surveyed as a railroad route. The road was improved during World War II to provide access to the Graysill Mine.

This mine produced the vanadium and uranium used in the first atomic bombs. It continued to supply these substances for this purpose until 1963. At its peak, there were 450 working claims in the area, but only about twenty men endured the harsh winters (not to mention the odorless, tasteless, radioactive radon gas), enabling the mine to remain in production year-round.

Description

The route commences in Silverton and follows US 550, the Million Dollar Highway, south for twenty-one miles to the Purgatory ski resort. The route passes through the resort and its network of paved roads without signs to guide you. An unpaved road exits the resort area and travels through the winter ski runs.

Numerous camping spots with good creek access lie off the road for about ten miles from the Purgatory ski resort.

Until the creek crossing 9.9 miles from the resort, the road is a well-maintained, unpaved, passenger-vehicle road. From this point, it gets narrower and rougher but remains an easy road for 4WD vehicles.

At the 16.1-mile point from Purgatory ski resort, the road passes the one remaining building (and a Forest Service information board) for the Graysill Mine. A mile and one-half further, past an attractive alpine lake, is Bolam Pass, at which point the road traverses a relatively level ridge through open meadows and patches of forest. This section affords pleasant views of adjoining hillsides and many wildflowers in the alpine meadows.

After about two miles, the road starts its descent and grows rougher, with considerable erosion evident. It is not difficult, but it does require caution.

Some twenty-two miles from the Purgatory ski resort, the road returns to easy passenger-vehicle conditions and follows Barlow Creek as it descends into the valley.

The trail ends when it intersects with Colorado 145, 5.3 miles south of Lizard Head Pass. On the opposite side of the highway is FR 535, which is Southwest #29: Fall Creek Trail.

Current Road Condition Information

San Juan National Forest
701 Camino del Rio
Durango, CO 81301
(970) 247-4874

Map References

USFS San Juan NF
USGS San Juan County
      La Plata County #2
      Dolores County #3
      San Miguel County #3
The Roads of Colorado, p. 130
Colorado Atlas & Gazetteer, p. 76

Route Directions

▼ 0.0   In front of the Silverton Visitor Center (at the intersection of Greene Street and US 550), zero trip meter and proceed south on US 550.
21.0 ▲   End at the Silverton Visitor Center.
           GPS: N 37°48.29' W 107°40.18'

▼ 21.0 TR Into Purgatory ski resort and zero trip meter.
0.0 ▲   Continue along US 550 toward Silverton.
            GPS: N 37°37.71' W 107°48.59'

▼ 0.0   Keep to the right.
8.4 ▲   TL Onto US 550. Zero trip meter.

▼ 0.3   SO Intersection. Dirt road enters from the right.
8.1 ▲   SO Intersection. Remain on paved road.

▼ 0.4   TR Paved road continues to the left. Follow unpaved road.
8.0 ▲   TL Onto paved road.

▼ 1.0   SO Hermosa Travel board to the right has a map posted. Sign to Bolam Pass.
7.4 ▲   BR Continue toward Purgatory Ski Resort.

▼ 2.1   BR Track on left.
6.3 ▲   BL Track on right.

▼ 3.1   BR Elbert Creek Road on left to Cafe de Los Piños. Follow Hermosa Creek Trail.
5.3 ▲   BL Elbert Creek Road on right to Cafe de Los Piños. Stay on main road.

▼ 3.5   BL Intersection. Remain on FR 578.
4.9 ▲   BR Intersection. Remain on FR 578.

▼ 4.4 SO Intersection.
4.0 ▲ SO Intersection.

▼ 4.8 SO Access to trout streams.
3.6 ▲ SO Access to trout streams.

▼ 6.6 SO USFS Sig Creek Campground.
1.8 ▲ SO USFS Sig Creek Campground.

▼ 6.7 SO Track on left.
1.7 ▲ SO Track on right.

▼ 7.5 SO Track on left to campsites.
0.9 ▲ SO Track on right to campsites.

▼ 7.6 SO Cross over creek.
0.8 ▲ SO Cross over creek.

▼ 8.4 SO Road on left crosses through East Fork of Hermosa Creek to Hermosa Creek Trailhead FR 577. Follow sign toward Bolam Pass. Zero trip meter.
0.0 ▲ Continue along route.
GPS: N 37°37.92' W 107°54.95'

▼ 0.0 Continue along main road.
7.9▲ Road on right. Zero trip meter.

▼ 0.4 SO Cattle guard.
7.5 ▲ SO Cattle guard.

▼ 0.7-1.6 SO Numerous campsites.
6.4-7.2 ▲ SO Numerous campsites.

▼ 1.5 SO Cross through creek.
6.4 ▲ SO Cross through creek.
GPS: N 37°38.80' W 107°55.65'

▼ 2.2 SO Intersection. FR 550 on left has signs to Rico and Hotel Draw via Scotch Creek. Follow FR 578 toward Bolam and Rico via Barlow Creek.
5.7 ▲ SO Intersection on right to Rico and Hotel Draw. Remain on FR 578.

▼ 2.9 SO Cattle guard.
3.4 ▲ SO Cattle guard.

▼ 3.5 SO Cross through creek.
4.4 ▲ SO Cross through creek.

SW Trail #28: Bolam Pass Trail

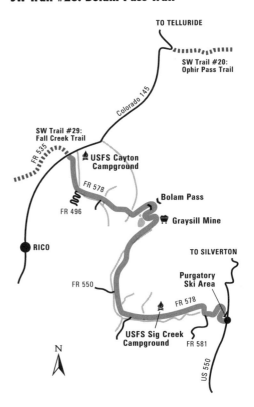

▼ 5.7 SO Cross over creek.
2.2 ▲ SO Cross over creek.

▼ 5.8 SO Cross through creek.
2.1 ▲ SO Cross through creek.

▼ 6.2 SO Cross over creek.
1.7 ▲ SO Cross over creek.

▼ 7.6 SO Cross over creek.
0.3 ▲ SO Cross over creek.

▼ 7.7 SO Graysill Mine ruins on right.
0.2 ▲ SO Graysill Mine ruins on left.

▼ 7.9 SO Cabin and historic marker. Zero trip meter.
0.0 ▲ Continue along main road.
GPS: N 37°42.82' W 107°53.93'

▼ 0.0 Continue along main road.

8.4 ▲	SO	Cabin and historic marker. Zero trip meter.

▼ 0.3	SO	Lake on left.
8.1 ▲	SO	Lake on right.

▼ 0.4	SO	Track on right is FR 578B.
8.0 ▲	SO	FR 578B on left.

▼ 1.4	SO	Bolam Pass summit (unmarked).
7.0 ▲	SO	Bolam Pass summit (unmarked).
		GPS: N 37°43.15' W 107°53.89'

▼ 2.3	TR	Cross over creek. Intersection.
6.1 ▲	TL	Intersection. Cross over creek.

▼ 4.6	SO	Cross through creek.
3.8 ▲	SO	Cross through creek.

▼ 4.8	SO	Track on left to creek.
3.6 ▲	SO	Track on right to creek.

▼ 5.0	SO	Cabin.
3.4 ▲	SO	Cabin.

▼ 5.8	SO	Cross over creek.
2.6 ▲	SO	Cross over creek.

▼ 5.9	SO	Intersection with FR 496 on left.
2.5 ▲	SO	Intersection with FR 496 on right.

▼ 6.9	SO	Barlow Lake on right.
1.5 ▲	SO	Barlow Lake on left.

▼ 8.1	BL	FR 476 Intersection on right. USFS Cayton Campground.
0.3 ▲	BR	USFS Cayton Campground. FR 476 on left.
		GPS: N 37°46.15' W 107°58.91'

▼ 8.4		Bridge over Dolores River. End at intersection with Colorado 145. Southwest #29: Fall Creek Trail is across Colorado 145.
0.0 ▲		At intersection of Colorado 145 and FR 578, zero trip meter and proceed along FR 578. Cross bridge over Dolores River.
		GPS: N 37°46.14' W 107°59.25'

Fall Creek Trail

STARTING POINT Intersection of Colorado 145 and County 57 P

FINISHING POINT Intersection of FR 535 and Colorado 145

TOTAL MILEAGE 48 6 miles

UNPAVED MILEAGE 47.7 miles

DRIVING TIME 3 hours

ROUTE ELEVATION 7,600 to 10,800 feet

USUALLY OPEN

DIFFICULTY RATING 2

SCENIC RATING 7

Special Attractions

- Long, but fairly easy, trail through Uncompahgre and San Juan National Forests.
- Relatively remote country, offering good backcountry camping.
- Numerous side roads, including many that are challenging to four-wheel drivers.
- Provides access for other activities, including good hiking, hunting, and fishing.
- Can connect with Southwest #28: Bolam Pass Trail.

Description

This route starts on paved road for the first mile and then becomes a maintained, gravel road until Woods Lake. The lake is a scenic fishing and picnic spot but overnight camping is not allowed. However, there are plenty of backcountry camping sites outside the immediate vicinity of the lake. From Woods Lake, the road narrows slightly but remains easy. You continue to drive through the forest of cottonwood, pine, spruce, and aspen trees. Along the road, after the passing the lake, there are some large stands of aspen that make for a particularly scenic drive in the fall.

As you continue towards Beaver Park, the forest opens up to a number of large meadows. When dry, the road remains easy, but there are sections that become quite boggy when wet. Most of the way navigation is easy. On occasion multiple forest side roads intersect within a short distance.

Other than in hunting season, when the area becomes a hive of activity, this route offers the opportunity for a solitary, tranquil journey through two of Colorado's magnificent national forests.

The end of the route intersects Colorado 145 and closely connects to Southwest #28: Bolam Pass Trail.

Current Road Condition Information
San Juan National Forest
701 Camino del Rio
Durango, CO 81301
(970) 247-4874

Map References
USFS   San Juan NF or Uncompahgre NF
USGS   Dolores #3
            San Miguel #3
Trails Illustrated, #141 (incomplete)
The Roads of Colorado, pp. 114, 130
Colorado Atlas & Gazetteer, p. 76

Route Directions

▼ 0.0   From Colorado 145 (northwest of Telluride), zero trip meter and proceed along County 57 P. This road is marked with a National Forest access sign to Fall Creek Road. Then cross bridge over the San Miguel River.
3.7 ▲   End at intersection with Colorado 145. Telluride is to the right.
            GPS: N 37°59.60′ W 108°01.28′

▼ 0.9   SO Cross over creek.
2.8 ▲   SO Cross over creek.

▼ 1.1   SO Picnic spot with grill on right.
2.6 ▲   SO Picnic spot with grill left.

▼ 3.7   BR Road forks. Proceed toward Woods Lake on 57 P (also FR 618). County Road 56 L goes to the left. Zero trip meter.
0.0 ▲   Continue along road.
            GPS: N 37°56.76′ W 108°02.16′

▼ 0.0   Continue toward the lake.
3.6 ▲   BR Onto County Road 57 P. Zero trip meter.

▼ 1.3   SO Enter Uncompahgre National Forest.
2.2 ▲   SO Leave Uncompahgre National Forest.

▼ 2.5   SO Track on right.
1.1 ▲   SO Track on left.

▼ 2.7   SO Cross bridge over creek.
0.9 ▲   SO Cross bridge over creek.

▼ 3.1   SO Small track on left.
0.5 ▲   SO Small track on right.

3.6   TR Intersection. Woods Lake is straight ahead. Zero trip meter and cross over creek.
0.0 ▲   Continue along main road toward Colorado 145.
            GPS: N 37°53.16′ W 108°03.23′

▼ 0.0   Continue along FR 618 toward Beaver Park.
11.3 ▲   TL Cross over creek, then T-intersection. Woods Lake is to the right. Zero trip meter.

▼ 0.6   SO Small track on right.
10.7 ▲   SO Small track on left.

▼ 1.7   SO Small track crosses the road.
9.5 ▲   SO Small track crosses the road.

▼ 3.6   BR Track on left.
7.7 ▲   BL Track on right.

▼ 4.8   SO Track on left.
6.5 ▲   SO Track on right.

▼ 6.3   SO Cross over McCulloch Creek.
5.0 ▲   SO Cross over McCulloch Creek.

▼ 7.2   SO Track on left.
4.1 ▲   SO Track on right.

▼ 8.0   SO Small track on right.
3.3 ▲   SO Small track on left.

SW Trail #29: Fall Creek Trail

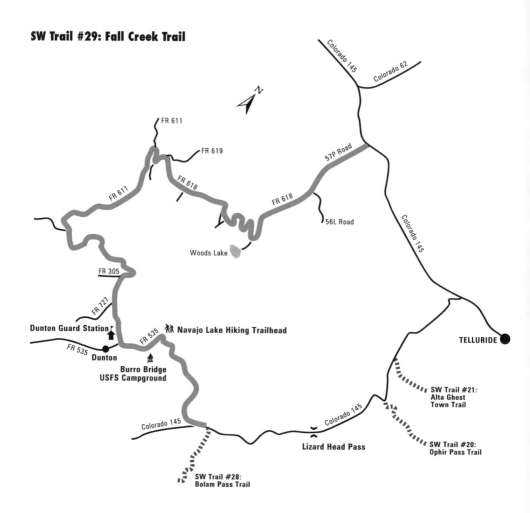

▼ 8.4   SO   Cattle guard.
2.9 ▲   SO   Cattle guard.

▼ 8.8   BL   Track on left.
2.5 ▲   BR   Track on right.

▼ 9.1   SO   Track on left.
2.2 ▲   SO   Track on right.

▼ 10.1   TL   FR 619 intersects on right. Then cross Main Beaver Creek.
1.2 ▲   TR   Cross Main Beaver Creek; FR 619 is straight ahead.
         GPS: N 37°53.41′ W 108°07.96′

▼ 10.6   TR   Intersection. Proceed toward Noorwood and Dunton. Lone Cone

Station is to the left.
0.7 ▲   TL   Lone Cone Station is straight ahead.
         GPS: N 37°53.37′ W 108°10.29′

▼ 10.9   SO   Cattle guard.
0.4 ▲   SO   Cattle guard.

▼ 11.3   TL   Intersection. Noorwood is to the right. Turn toward Dunton onto FR 611 and zero trip meter.
0.0 ▲   Continue along FR 618.
         GPS: N 37°53.95′ W 108°10.17′

▼ 0.0   Continue along FR 611.
9.3 ▲   TR   Turn onto FR 618.

▼ 0.6   SO   Cross bridge over Beaver Creek.
8.6 ▲   SO   Cross bridge over Beaver Creek.

▼ 0.8　SO　Cattle guard.
8.5 ▲　SO　Cattle guard.

▼ 3.3　SO　Track on left, then track on right.
6.0 ▲　SO　Track on left, then track on right.

▼ 4.8　SO　Cross over creek.
4.5 ▲　SO　Cross over creek.

▼ 4.9　SO　Track on right is FR 611.2.
4.3 ▲　　　Track on left is FR 611.2.

▼ 5.6　SO　Cross over creek. Track on left.
3.7 ▲　　　Track on right. Cross over creek.
　　　　GPS: N 37°52.06′ W 108°09.48′

▼ 5.7　SO　Track on right.
3.6 ▲　SO　Track on left.

▼ 7.1　SO　Track on right.
2.2 ▲　SO　Track on left.

▼ 9.3　SO　Fork in road.
0.1 ▲　SO　Track enters on left.
　　　　GPS: N 37°49.05′ W 108°11.31′

▼ 9.4　BL　Intersection. Zero trip meter and follow FR 611.
0.0 ▲　　　Continue along FR 611.
　　　　GPS: N 37°48.98′ W 108°11.15′

▼ 0.0　　　Continue along FR 611 and pass track on right.
10.9 ▲　BR　Track on left. Then road forks; stay to the right. Zero trip meter.

▼ 2.8　SO　Cross over creek.
8.1 ▲　SO　Cross over creek.

▼ 4.7　SO　Track on left.
6.2 ▲　SO　Track on right.

▼ 6.3　SO　Track on left. Cross creek.
4.6 ▲　BL　Cross creek. Then track on right.

▼ 7.1　SO　FR 305 on right.
3.8 ▲　SO　FR 305 on left.

▼ 7.8　SO　Track on left.

3.1 ▲　SO　Track on right.

▼ 8.7　SO　Cattle guard; then FR 727 on right.
2.2 ▲　SO　FR 727 on left; then cattle guard.

▼ 10.8　SO　Cattle guard. Then track to cabin on right.
0.1 ▲　SO　Track to cabin on left. Cattle guard.

▼ 10.95　TL　Intersection with FR 535. Zero trip meter at intersection and cross over creek.
0.0 ▲　　　Continue on FR 611.
　　　　GPS: N 37°46.83′ W 108°05.32′

▼ 0.0　　　Proceed along FR 535.
9.7 ▲　TR　Cross over creek. Zero trip meter at intersection and turn onto FR 611 (Black Mesa Road).

▼ 1.25　SO　USFS Burro Bridge Campground on right.
8.4 ▲　SO　USFS Burro Bridge Campground on left.

▼ 1.9　SO　Cross Burro Bridge over Dolores River.
7.7 ▲　SO　Cross Burro Bridge over Dolores River.

▼ 2.3　SO　Cross over Meadow Creek.
7.4 ▲　SO　Cross over Meadow Creek.

▼ 2.6　SO　Short track on left to Navajo Trailhead.
7.1 ▲　SO　Short track on right to Navajo Trailhead.

▼ 4.7　SO　Track on left to Kilpacker Trailhead.
5.0 ▲　SO　Track on right to Kilpacker Trailhead.

▼ 4.8　SO　Private cabin on left.
4.8 ▲　SO　Private cabin on right.

▼ 5.5　SO　FR 471 on right passes Calico Trailhead.
4.1 ▲　SO　FR 471 on left passes Calico Trailhead

▼ 5.7　SO　Cross over Coal Creek.

3.9 ▲   SO Cross over Coal Creek.

▼ 8.1   SO Track on left at switchback.
1.6 ▲   SO Track on right at switchback.

▼ 9.7   End at intersection with
          Colorado 145.
0.0 ▲   From Colorado 145 (5.3 miles south
          of Lizard Head Pass), zero trip meter
          and turn onto FR 535 toward
          Dunton.
          N 37°46.34' W 107°58.84'

SOUTHWEST REGION TRAIL #30

Uncompahgre Plateau Trail

STARTING POINT Intersection of US 550 and
   Jay Jay Road, north of Montrose
FINISHING POINT Intersection of Colorado 141
   and County 26.10 (FR 402)
TOTAL MILEAGE 90.3 miles
UNPAVED MILEAGE 85.6 miles
DRIVING TIME 4 hours
ROUTE ELEVATION 5,597 to 9,120 feet
USUALLY OPEN Mid-June to late November
DIFFICULTY RATING 2
SCENIC RATING 7

Special Attractions

■ Expansive views from the Uncompahgre
  Plateau, particularly from Windy Point.
■ An extensive network of 4WD trails.
■ Good backcountry camping.

History

Columbine Pass, named for the Colorado
state flower, which used to grow in abundance here, is located on the Uncompahgre
Plateau and was crossed by the Hayden
Survey expedition in the mid-1870s. The
plateau was an important summer hunting
ground for the Ute for thousands of years
prior to the Washington Treaty of 1880,
when they ceded the entire area and were
relocated to reservations.

Description

This route starts at the intersection of US
550 and Jay Jay Road, 4.7 miles northwest of
the National Forest office in Montrose (2505
S. Townsend). The next five miles involves a
considerable number of intersections, so care
is necessary to navigate correctly. At the end
this section of the route, you should turn on
to Rim Road. There are more-direct routes
from Montrose, but this route offers the
more varied and interesting views.

Initially, Rim Road is a well-maintained,
wide 2WD road that provides some good
views over the local ranch land and the San
Juan Mountains in the distance to the south.
There are also numerous small side roads: stay
on the main road in each case. Further along
the road, there are some sections that are rocky,
but they will not pose any problems. The road
travels along the rim of a canyon and provides
good views down to the floor below.

After turning on to FR 402 (Divide
Road), you will pass numerous camping
sites, which are heavily used in hunting season, and an extensive network of 4WD side
roads, many of which can be very muddy.
FR 402 is wide and well maintained and
suitable for passenger vehicles in dry conditions. The views to the west, down into the
valley below, are particularly scenic.

As you descend from Uncompahgre
Plateau, the scenery changes to the red rock
walls of Jacks Canyon before connecting
with Colorado 141 in the vast Unaweep

Jacks Canyon

View from Rim Road into Dry Creek Basin

Canyon. From here, the road travels along the path of East Creek before crossing the Gunnison River and joining US 50. Gunnison is approximately twenty-four miles from the intersection with Colorado 141, at the start of the paved road.

Current Road Condition Information
Uncompahgre National Forest
Ouray Ranger District
2505 South Townsend
Montrose, CO 81401
(970) 240-5300

Map References
USFS   Uncompahgre NF
USGS   Montrose County #1
　　　　Montrose County #2
　　　　Mesa County #6
The Roads of Colorado, pp. 81, 97–98, 114
Colorado Atlas & Gazetteer, pp. 54–56, 65–66

Route Directions

▼ 0.0　　At intersection of US 550 and Jay Jay Road, turn west (left, if coming from Montrose).

5.0 ▲　　End at intersection with US 550.
　　　　GPS: N 38°31.91′ W 107°56.19′

▼ 0.1　SO Cross railroad tracks. Name of road changes to Menoken Road.
4.9 ▲　SO Cross railroad tracks.

▼ 1.4　SO Cross over bridge and then a second bridge.
3.6 ▲　SO Cross over two bridges.

▼ 1.6　BL Fork in road; go left onto South River Road.
3.4 ▲　BR At fork in the road.

▼ 2.0　BR County 5975 is on the left.
3.0 ▲　BL County 5975 is on the right.

▼ 2.9　BL Intersection. Remain on paved road.
2.1 ▲　BR Intersection.

▼ 3.5　TL Stop sign at intersection. Turn onto County 5850.
1.5 ▲　TR Intersection. Turn onto South River Road.
　　　　GPS: N 38°31.56′ W 107°59.68′

▼ 3.9　TR Onto Kiowa Road.

1.1 ▲   TL   Onto County 5850.

▼ 4.7   BL   Bear left, then cross bridge. Bear left
             again onto unpaved road named
             Shavano Valley Road.

0.2 ▲   BR   Onto Kiowa Road. Then cross bridge
             and bear left again.

▼ 5.0   TR   Onto Rim Road. Zero trip meter.

0.0 ▲   Continue to the left.
             GPS: N 38°30.92' W 108°00.54'

▼ 0.0   Proceed along Rim Road.

13.1 ▲   TL   Intersection. Zero trip meter.

▼ 1.7   SO   Track crosses road.

11.4 ▲   SO   Track crosses road.

▼ 2.2   SO   Track on right.

10.9 ▲   SO   Track on left.

▼ 2.5   SO   Track on right. Note: From this point,
             there will be numerous side tracks, but
             remain on Rim Road.

10.7 ▲   SO   Track on left.

▼ 3.0   SO   Track on right goes into canyon.

10.2 ▲   SO   Track on left goes into canyon. Note:
             From this point, there will be numerous
             side tracks, but remain on Rim Road.
             GPS: N 38°29.14' W 108°02.50'

▼ 5.7   SO   Cross under high voltage wires and
             cross cattle guard.

7.5 ▲   SO   Cattle guard. Cross under high voltage
             wires.

▼ 9.7   BL   Cattleyards on left, then fork in road.

3.5 ▲   BR   Fork in the road, then cattleyards on
             right.

▼ 12.2   SO   Cattleyards on left, then cattle guard.

0.9 ▲   SO   Cattle guard, then cattleyards on right.
             GPS: N 38°24.43' W 108°04.21'

▼ 13.1   TR   T-intersection with Old Highway 90.
             Turn right and go through seasonal clo-
             sure gate. Zero trip meter.

0.0 ▲   Turn onto Rim Road.
             GPS: N 38°21.79' W 108°02.94'

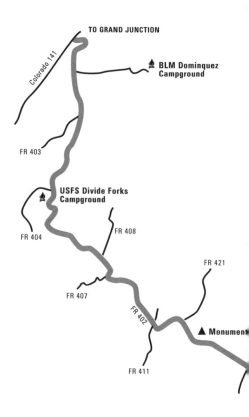

▼ 0.0   Proceed along Old Highway 90.

23.6 ▲   TL   Intersection. Zero trip meter.

▼ 0.4   SO   Cross over East Fork of Dry Creek.

23.2   SO   Cross over East Fork of Dry Creek.

▼ 5.8   SO   USFS Silesca Ranger Station on left.

17.8 ▲   SO   USFS Silesca Ranger Station on right.

▼ 7.9   SO   FR 402 on left (Dave Wood Road and
             Norwood).

15.7 ▲   SO   FR 402 on right.
             GPS: N 38°19.02' W 108°09.21'

▼ 8.3   SO   USFS Iron Springs Campground on left.

15.2 ▲   SO   USFS Iron Springs Campground on
             right.

▼ 8.5   BR   Old Highway 90 turns left.

15.0 ▲   BL   Intersection: Old Highway 90.

SW Trail #30: Uncompahgre Plateau Trail

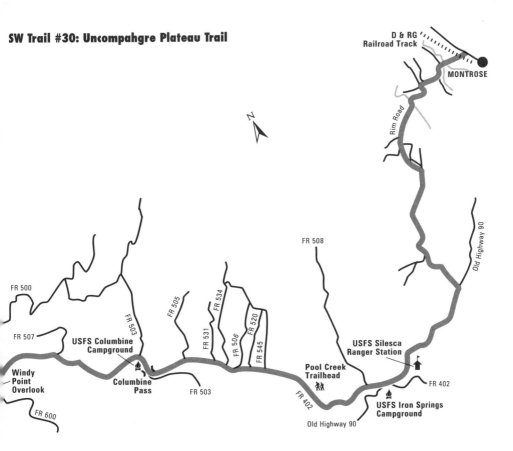

▼ 8.8   SO FR 527 on right.
14.7 ▲ SO FR 527 on left.

▼ 9.5   SO Road on right is Transfer Road/FR 508
            to Olathe.
14.0 ▲ SO FR 508 on left.

▼ 10.9 SO West Antone Spring on left.
12.7 ▲ SO West Antone Spring on right.

▼ 11.9 SO Road to Pool Creek on right.
11.6 ▲ SO Road to Pool Creek on left.

▼ 13.7 SO Pool Creek Trailhead on right.
9.9 ▲   SO Pool Creek Trailhead on left.

▼ 14.0 SO West Pool Creek on right.
9.5 ▲   SO West Pool Creek on left.

▼ 15.2 SO FR 546 on right.
8.3 ▲   SO FR 546 on left.

▼ 16.3 SO FR 545 on right.
7.3 ▲   SO FR 545 on left.

▼ 17.5 SO FR 520 on right to Long Creek.
6.0 ▲   SO FR 520 on left to Long Creek.

▼ 18.2 SO FR 506 on right to Payne Mesa.
5.4 ▲   SO FR 506 on left to Payne Mesa.

▼ 18.7 SO Cattleyards on left. FR 534 on right.
4.9 ▲   SO FR 534 on left. Cattleyards on right.

▼ 19.7 SO FR 531 to Moore Mesa on right.
3.9 ▲   SO FR 531 to Moore Mesa on left.

▼ 21.2 SO FR 505 on right.
2.4 ▲   SO FR 505 on left.

▼ 22.8 SO USFS Tabeguache scenic overlook on
            left.
0.7 ▲   SO USFS Tabeguache scenic overlook on
            right.

▼ 23.6　BR　Columbine Pass. FR 503 and cattle-
　　　　　yards are on left. Zero trip meter.
0.0 ▲　　　Continue on FR 402 to the left.
GPS: N 38°25.00′ W 108°22.86′

▼ 0.0　　　Continue on FR 402 to the right.
33.6 ▲　BL　Columbine Pass. FR 503 and cattle-
　　　　　yards are on left. Zero trip meter.

▼ 0.3　　SO　FR 533 to Monitor Mesa on the right.
33.2 ▲　SO　FR 533 to Monitor Mesa on the left.

▼ 0.7　　SO　USFS Columbine Campground on left.
32.9 ▲　SO　USFS Columbine Campground on right.

▼ 0.9　　TL　Cattle guard, then cross through creek
　　　　　to intersection. Follow FR 402 toward
　　　　　Windy Point. To the right is FR 503,
　　　　　Delta-Nucla Road.
32.7 ▲　TR　Intersection. FR 503 to Delta-Nucla is
　　　　　to the left. Turn right toward Columbine
　　　　　Pass. Cross creek, then cattle guard.
GPS: N 38°25.70′ W 108°22.89′

▼ 2.4　　SO　Track on right.
31.1 ▲　SO　Track on left.

▼ 3.1　　SO　FR 529 to Sawmill Mesa on right.
30.5 ▲　SO　FR 529 to Sawmill Mesa on left.

▼ 6.5　　SO　FR 507, Lockhart on right.
27.1 ▲　SO　FR 507, Lockhart on left.

▼ 10.9　SO　FR 600 on left.
22.7 ▲　SO　FR 600 on right.

▼ 11.1　SO　Windy Point (great views!) on left.
22.5 ▲　SO　Windy Point (great views!) on right.

▼ 13.3　SO　FR 500 on right.
20.3 ▲　SO　FR 500 on left.

▼ 14.3　SO　Cattleyards on right.
19.3 ▲　SO　Cattleyards on left.

▼ 16.4　SO　Track on left.
17.2 ▲　SO　Track on right.

▼ 17.8　SO　Monument Hill on right.

15.7 ▲　SO　Monument Hill on left.

▼ 19.5　SO　Long Point and FR 421 on right.
14.0 ▲　SO　Long Point and FR 421 on left.

▼ 21.3　SO　FR 411 on left, then cattle guard.
12.3 ▲　SO　Cattle guard, then FR 411 on right.

▼ 21.6　SO　Short track on right.
12.0 ▲　SO　Short track on left.

▼ 23.0　SO　Uncompahgre Butte on right.
10.5 ▲　SO　Uncompahgre Butte on left.

▼ 24.2　SO　Track on right.
9.3 ▲　SO　Track on left.

▼ 25.0　SO　3 H on left.
8.6 ▲　SO　3 H on right.

▼ 25.8　SO　Mesa Creek FR 407 on left.
7.8 ▲　SO　Mesa Creek FR 407 on right.

▼ 27.3　SO　FR 408 on right.
6.3 ▲　SO　FR 408 on left.

▼ 28.2　SO　3 J on right dead-ends.
5.4 ▲　SO　3 J on left dead-ends.

▼ 29.2　SO　FR 410 on left dead-ends.
4.4 ▲　SO　FR 410 on right dead-ends.

▼ 29.4　SO　Track on right to USFS Cold Springs
　　　　　Work Center.
4.2 ▲　SO　Track on left to USFS Cold Springs
　　　　　Work Center.

▼ 31.0　SO　Track and cattleyards on left.
2.5 ▲　SO　Cattleyards and track on right.

▼ 33.4　SO　USFS Divide Forks Campground on
　　　　　left.
0.2 ▲　SO　USFS Divide Forks Campground on
　　　　　right.

▼ 33.6　SO　FR 404 Uranium Road on left. Zero trip
　　　　　meter.
0.0 ▲　　　Continue along FR 402.
GPS: N 38°41.21′ W 108°41.18′

▼ 0.0		Continue along FR 402.
15.0 ▲	SO	FR 404 Uranium Road on right. Zero trip meter.

▼ 2.9	SO	Cattle guard.
12.1 ▲	SO	Cattle guard.

▼ 5.4	SO	FR 403 to Big Creek Reservoir on left.
9.6 ▲	SO	FR 403 to Big Creek Reservoir on right.

▼ 7.0	SO	Cattle guard.
8.0 ▲	SO	Cattle guard.

▼ 8.8	SO	USFS Uncompahgre information board, seasonal closure gate, and cattle guard.
6.2 ▲	SO	Cattle guard. Seasonal closure gate and USFS Uncompahgre information board.

▼ 9.2	SO	Dominquez State Wildlife area on right and road to Dominquez BLM campground.
5.8 ▲	SO	Dominquez State Wildlife area on left and road to Dominquez BLM campground.

▼ 12.9	SO	Cattle guard.
2.1 ▲	SO	Cattle guard.

▼ 15.0		Cattle guard. End at intersection with Colorado 141.
0.0 ▲		At intersection of County 90 and Colorado 141, zero trip meter and proceed along County 90. Cross cattle guard.

GPS: N 38°50.26′ W 108°34.45′

Owl Creek and Chimney Rock Trail

STARTING POINT Intersection US 550 and County 10 near Ridgway
FINISHING POINT Intersection County 858 and US 50
TOTAL MILEAGE 40.9 miles
UNPAVED MILEAGE 40.9 miles

DRIVING TIME 2 hours
ROUTE ELEVATION 7,000 to 10,200 feet
USUALLY OPEN May to November
DIFFICULTY RATING 1
SCENIC RATING 8

Special Attractions

■ An easy trail that provides a more interesting route than the paved road when traveling between Ouray and Gunnison.
■ Views of Chimney Peak and Courthouse Mountain.
■ Scenic Silver Jack Reservoir.
■ Access to good hiking, fishing, and backcountry camping.

Description

This route, on maintained gravel roads across mainly gentle grades, starts just north of Ridgway at the intersection of US 550 and County 10. Initially, the road travels through ranch land before crossing Cimarron Ridge at Owl Creek Pass and continuing through

Chimney Rock

A stand of aspens and a rock outcrop near Silver Jack Reservoir

Uncompahgre National Forest.

The route offers many good views of the conspicuous rock peaks known as Chimney Rock and Courthouse Mountain. Many large stands of aspen line the route, providing wonderful fall scenery for photographers or for those who just enjoy the bright yellow panorama so typical of Colorado.

The road continues its gentle course past Silver Jack Reservoir and through to US 50.

Current Road Condition Information
Uncompahgre National Forest
Ouray Ranger District
2505 South Townsend
Montrose, CO 8140
(970) 240-5300

Map References
USFS Uncompahgre NF
USGS Ouray County #1
　　　　Gunnison #6
Trails Illustrated, #141 (incomplete)
The Roads of Colorado, pp. 115, 99
Colorado Atlas & Gazetteer, pp. 66–67

Route Directions

▼ 0.0　　From US 550 (1.7 miles north of the junction with Colorado 62 in Ridgway and approximately 26 miles south of Montrose), zero trip meter and proceed east along County Road 10. This turn-off is marked with a National Forest Access sign to Owl Creek Pass.

8.6 ▲　　End at intersection with US 550. This intersection is 12 miles north of Ouray.
　　　　GPS: N 38°10.44′ W 107°44.47′

▼ 0.8　BL　Road forks.
7.7 ▲　BR　Intersection.

▼ 2.5　BL　Cow Creek goes to the right.
6.1 ▲　BR　Cow Creek goes to the left.

▼ 3.9　BR　County 8 enters on left.
4.7 ▲　BL　Remain on County Road 10 toward Ridgway and US 550.

▼ 4.9　SO　Bridge over creek.
3.7 ▲　SO　Bridge over creek.

▼ 5.3 BL Road forks. Turn onto County 8 toward Owl Creek Pass.

3.3 ▲ BR Onto County Road 10.

▼ 5.6 SO Cattle guard.

3.0 ▲ SO Cattle guard.

▼ 6.1 SO Cattle guard

2.5 ▲ SO Cattle guard.

▼ 6.8 SO Cattle guard. Road narrows.

1.8 ▲ SO Cattle guard.

▼ 7.7 SO Cattle guard. Enter Uncompahgre National Forest. Name of road becomes FR 858.

0.9 ▲ SO Leave Uncompahgre National Forest, then cross cattle guard.

▼ 8.6 BL Vista Point scenic overlook on right. Zero trip meter.

0.0 ▲ Continue toward Ridgway.
GPS: N 38°11.21′ W 107°37.74′

▼ 0.0 Continue toward Owl Creek Pass.

6.6 ▲ BR Vista Point scenic overlook on left. Zero trip meter.

▼ 0.3 SO Road on right.

6.3 ▲ SO Road on left.

▼ 2.7 SO Track on left.

3.8 ▲ SO Track on right.

▼ 3.4 SO Cattle guard.

3.2 ▲ SO Cattle guard.

▼ 4.0 BL Track on right dead-ends in short distance.

2.5 ▲ BR Track on left dead-ends in short distance.

▼ 5.9 SO Cross over Nate Creek Ditch.

0.6 ▲ SO Cross over Nate Creek Ditch.

▼ 6.6 SO Cattle guard; then Owl Creek Pass. Track on left goes to parking bay. Zero trip meter at summit.

0.0 ▲ Continue along main road toward Ridgway.
GPS: N 38°09.45′ W 107°33.71′

SW Trail #31: Owl Creek and Chimney Rock Trail

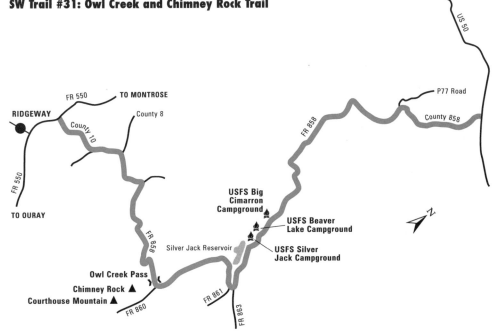

▼ 0.0   Continue along FR 858.

6.6 ▲   SO Owl Creek Pass. Track on right goes to a small parking area. Zero trip meter at the summit and cross over cattle guard.

▼ 0.3   BL Track on right is FR 860, which offers several viewing areas for Chimney Rock.

6.3 ▲   BR Track on left is FR 860. Remain on FR 858 toward Owl Creek Pass.

▼ 0.8   SO Cattle guard.

5.8 ▲   SO Cattle guard.

2.9   SO Cross over bridge.

3.7 ▲   SO Cross over bridge

▼ 5.0   SO Cattle guard.

1.6 ▲   SO Cattle guard.

▼ 6.3   SO Cimarron Fork track on left.

0.3 ▲   SO Track to Cimarron Fork on right.

▼ 6.4   SO Cross over bridge.

0.2 ▲   SO Cross over bridge.

▼ 6.5   SO Track on right to Middle Fork (FR 861.1) Trailhead. Cross over bridge.

0.1 ▲   SO Cross over bridge. Track on left goes to Middle Fork Trailhead.

▼ 6.6   TL Follow FR 858 toward Cimarron and Silver Jack Reservoir. Right goes to East Fork Trailhead. Zero trip meter.

0.0 ▲   Continue toward Owl Creek Pass.
         GPS: N 38°12.32' W 107°30.92'

▼ 0.0   Continue along FR 858.

19.1 ▲   TR Straight goes to East Fork Trailhead. Zero trip meter.

▼ 0.8   SO Cross cattle guard with fishing access on left.

18.3 ▲   SO Fishing access on right. Cross cattle guard.

▼ 1.7   SO Alpine Trailhead on right.

17.4 ▲   SO Alpine Trailhead on left.

▼ 2.3   SO FR 838 on right and Silver Jack Reservoir overlook on left.

16.8 ▲   SO Overlook to Silver Jack Reservoir on right and FR 838 on left.

▼ 2.6   SO USFS Silver Jack Campground on left.

16.5 ▲   SO USFS Silver Jack Campground on right.

▼ 3.9   SO USFS Beaver Lake Campground on left.

15.2 ▲   SO USFS Beaver Lake Campground on right.

▼ 4.6   SO USFS Big Cimarron Campground on left. Paddock on right; then cattle guard. Cross bridge and leave the Uncompahgre National Forest. Road is now County 858.

14.5 ▲   SO Enter Uncompahgre National Forest and road becomes FR 858. Cross bridge and cattle guard. USFS Big Cimarron Campground on right.

▼ 5.4   SO Cross over bridge.

13.7 ▲   SO Cross over bridge.

▼ 9.0   SO Cross over bridge.

10.1 ▲   SO Cross over bridge.

▼ 10.7   SO Cross over bridge.

8.4 ▲   SO Cross over bridge.

▼ 11.4   SO Cross over bridge.

7.7 ▲   SO Cross over bridge.

▼ 13.4   SO County Road P 77 on left.

5.7 ▲   SO County Road P 77 on right.

▼ 17.2   SO Cross over bridge.

1.9 ▲   SO Cross over bridge.

▼ 19.1   End at intersection with US 50.

0.0 ▲   From US 50 (approximately 40 miles west of Gunnison) at the National Forest Access sign to Cimarron Road and Silver Jack Reservoir, zero trip meter and proceed southbound along Cimarron Road (County Road 858).
         GPS: N 38°24.86' W 107°31.57'

Selected Further Readings

Massey, Peter and Jeanne Wilson. *4WD Adventures: Colorado*. Castle Rock, Colo.: Swagman Publishing Inc., 1999.

Massey, Peter and Jeanne Wilson. *4WD Trails: North-Central Colorado*. Castle Rock, Colo.: Swagman Publishing Inc., 1999.

Massey, Peter and Jeanne Wilson. *4WD Trails: South-Central Colorado*. Castle Rock, Colo.: Swagman Publishing Inc., 1999.

Abbott, Carl, Stephen J. Leonard, and David McComb. *Colorado: A History of the Centennial State*. Niwot, Colo.: University Press of Colorado, 1994.

Aldrich, John K. *Ghosts of the Eastern San Juans*. Lakewood, Colo.: Centennial Graphics, 1987.

Aldrich, John K. *Ghosts of the Western San Juans*. Vols. 1 and 2. Lakewood, Colo.: Centennial Graphics, 1991.

Bancroft, Caroline. *Colorful Colorado*. Boulder, Colo.: Johnson Books, 1987.

Bancroft, Caroline. *Unique Ghost Towns and Mountain Spots*. Boulder, Colo.: Johnson Books, 1961.

Bauer, Carolyn. *Colorado Ghost Towns— Colorado Traveler Guidebooks*. Frederick, Colo.: Renaissance House, 1987.

Beckner, Raymond M. *Along the Colorado Trail*. Pueblo, Colo.: O'Brien Printing & Stationery, 1975.

Benham, Jack. *Ouray*. Ouray, Colo.: Bear Creek Publishing, 1976.

Boyd, Leanne C. and H. Glenn Carson. *Atlas of Colorado Ghost Towns*. Vols. 1 and 2. Deming, N.M.: Carson Enterprises, Ltd., 1984.

Bright, William. *Colorado Place Names*. Boulder, Colo.: Johnson Books, 1993.

Brown, Robert L. *Colorado Ghost Towns Past & Present*. Caldwell, Idaho: Caxton Printers, Ltd., 1972.

Brown, Robert L. *Ghost Towns of the Colorado Rockies*. Caldwell, Idaho: Caxton Printers, Ltd., 1990.

Brown, Robert L. *Jeep Trails to Colorado Ghost Towns*. Caldwell, Idaho: Caxton Printers, Ltd., 1995.

Bueler, Gladys R. *Colorado's Colorful Characters*. Boulder, Colo.: Pruett Publishing, 1981.

Carver, Jack, Jerry Vondergeest, Dallas Boyd, and Tom Pade. *Land of Legend*. Denver, Colo.: Caravon Press, 1959.

Crofutt, George A. *Crofutt's Grip-Sack Guide of Colorado*. Omaha: Overland Publishing, 1885. Reprinted, Boulder, Colo.: Johnson Books, 1981.

Cromie, Alice. *A Tour Guide to the Old West*. Nashville, Tenn.: Rutledge Hill Press, 1990.

Crutchfield, James A. *It Happened in Colorado*. Helena & Billings, Mont.: Falcon Press Publishing, 1993.

Dallas, Sandra. *Colorado Ghost Towns and Mining Camps*. Norman, Okla.: University of Oklahoma Press, 1985.

DeLong, Brad. *4-Wheel Freedom*. Boulder, Colo.: Paladin Press, 1996.

Dorset, Phyllis Flanders. *The New Eldorado: The Story of Colorado's Gold & Silver Rushes*. New York: Macmillan, 1970.

Eberhart, Perry. *Guide to the Colorado Ghost Towns and Mining Camps*. Chicago, Ill.: Swallow Press, 1995.

Fisher, Vardis, and Opal Laurel Holmes. *Gold Rushes and Mining Camps of the Early American West*. Caldwell, Idaho: Caxton Printers, Ltd., 1968.

Florin, Lambert. *Ghost Towns of the West.* New York: Promontory Press, 1993.

Foster, Mike. *Strange Genius: The Life of Ferdinand Vandeveer Hayden.* Niwot, Colo.: Roberts Rinehart Publishers, 1994.

Green, Stewart M. *Bureau of Land Management Back Country Byways.* Helena, Mont.: Falcon Press, 1995.

Gregory, Lee. *Colorado Scenic Guide: Southern Region.* Boulder, Colo.: Johnson Books, 1990.

Heck, Larry E. *4-Wheel Drive Roads & Ghost Towns of the San Juans.* Aurora, Colo.: Pass Patrol, 1995.

Helmuth, Ed and Gloria. *The Passes of Colorado.* Boulder, Colo.: Pruett Publishing, 1994.

Hilton, George W. *American Narrow Gauge Railroads.* Stanford: Stanford University Press.

Jessen, Ken. *Colorado Gunsmoke: True Stories of Outlaws and Lawmen on the Colorado Frontier.* Loveland, Colo.: J. V. Publications, 1986.

Koch, Don. *The Colorado Pass Book.* Boulder, Colo.: Pruett Publishing, 1992.

McTighe, James. *Roadside History of Colorado.* Boulder, Colo.: Johnson Books, 1984.

Noel, Thomas J., Paul F. Mahoney, and Richard E. Stevens. *Historical Atlas of Colorado.* Norman, Okla.: University of Oklahoma Press, 1994.

Norton, Boyd and Barbara. *Backroads of Colorado.* Stillwater, Minn: Voyageur Press, 1995.

Ormes, Robert M. *Railroads and the Rockies.* Denver, Colo.: Sage Books, 1963.

Ormes, Robert. *Tracking Ghost Railroads in Colorado.* Colorado Springs, Colo.: Green Light Graphics, 1992.

O'Rourke, Paul M. *Frontier in Transition: A History of Southwestern Colorado.* Denver, Colo.: Bureau of Land Management, 1980.

Parker, Ben H., Jr. *Gold Panning and*

Placering in Colorado. Denver, Colo.: U.S. Geological Survey, Department of Natural Resources, 1992.

Pettem, Silvia. *Colorado Mountains & Passes—Colorado Traveler Guidebooks.* Frederick, Colo.: Renaissance House, 1991.

Pettit, Jan. *Utes: The Mountain People.* Boulder, Colo.: Johnson Books, 1994.

Pritchard, Sandra F. *Men, Mining & Machines.* Dillon, Colo.: Summit County Historical Society, 1996.

Reidhead, Darlene A. *Tour the San Juans. Vols. 1 and 2.* Cortez, Colo.: Southwest Printing.

Sagstetter, Beth and Bill. *The Mining Camps Speak.* Denver, Colo.: BenchMark Publishing of Colorado, 1998.

Sinnotte, Barbara. *Colorado: A Guide to the State & National Parks.* Edison, N.J.: Hunter, 1996.

Smith, Duane A. *Colorado Mining: A Photographic History.* Albuquerque, N.M.: University of New Mexico Press, 1977.

Southworth, Dave. *Colorado Mining Camps.* Wild Horse, 1997.

Southworth, Dave. *Gunfighters of the Old West.* Wild Horse, 1997.

Taylor, Colin F. *The Plains Indians.* New York: Barnes & Noble Books and Salamander Books, 1997.

Ubbelohde, Carl, Maxine Benson, and Duane A. Smith. *A Colorado History.* Boulder, Colo.: Pruett Publishing, 1995.

Waldman, Carl. *Encyclopedia of Native American Tribes.* New York: Facts on File, 1988.

Wilkins, Tivis E. *Colorado Railroads Chronological Development.* Boulder, Colo.: Pruett Publishing, 1974.

Wilson, Ray D. *Colorado Historical Tour Guide.* Carpentersville, Ill.: Crossroads Communications, 1990.

Wolle, Muriel Sibell. *The Bonanza Trail.* Chicago, Ill.: The Swallow Press, 1953.

About the Authors

Peter Massey grew up in the outback of Australia. After retiring from a career in investment banking at the age of thirty-five, he served as a director of a number of companies in the United States, the United Kingdom, and Australia. He moved to Colorado in 1993.

Jeanne Wilson was born and grew up in Washington, D.C. She lived and worked in New York City as a young adult and has been a resident of Colorado since 1993.

Traveling extensively in Australia, Europe, Asia, and Africa, the authors covered more than 80,000 miles touring throughout the United States and outback Australia in the past five years. They traveled more than 15,000 miles in Colorado to research their books.

The authors' first book, *4WD Adventures: Colorado,* is a compilation of more than 70 exciting and interesting trails in Colorado. The fully illustrated volume includes detailed information about Colorado towns, ghost towns, historical characters, wildlife, and wildflowers that relate to each route. Their set of three new books, *4WD Trails: North-Central Colorado, 4WD Trails: South-Central Colorado,* and *4WD Trails: Southwest Colorado,* covers three of the regions found in *4WD Adventures: Colorado.*

Information on all these books can be found on the Internet at www.4wdbooks.com.

Photographic Credits

Unless otherwise indicated in the following list of acknowledgments (which is organized by page number), all photographs were taken by Peter Massey and are copyrighted by Swagman Publishing, Inc., or by Peter Massey.

Page 20: Denver Public Library Western History Collection. *Page 29:* Denver Public Library Western History Collection. *Page 38:* Denver Public Library Western History Collection, by William Henry Jackson. *Page 39:* (upper) Denver Public Library Western History Collection. (lower) Denver Public Library Western History Collection, by Muriel Sibell Wolle. *Page 46:* Denver Public Library Western History Collection. *Page 67:* (lower) Denver Public Library Western History Collection. *Page 71:* (lower) Denver Public Library Western History Collection. *Page 78:* Colorado Historical Society. *Page 83:* (lower) Denver Public Library Western History Collection, by Jesse L. Nusbaum. *Page 84:* Denver Public Library Western History Collection, by George L. Beam. *Page 87:* (lower) Denver Public Library Western History Collection. *Page 90:* Denver Public Library Western History Collection, by Louis Charles McClure. *Page 105:* Denver Public Library Western History Collection, by George L. Beam. *Page 107:* Beth and Bill Sagstetter, BenchMark Publishing.

ORDER FORM

To purchase any of our 4WD books, contact your local book or map store or order direct from Swagman Publishing by any of the following methods:

Telephone orders: **800-660-5107**
Or fax your order: **303-688-4388**
Or order on-line: **www.4wdbooks.com**
Or mail your order to this address: **Swagman Publishing, Inc.**
P.O. Box 519
Castle Rock, CO 80104

- -

I understand that I may return any book for a full refund—for any reason, no questions asked.

	Price	Quantity	Total
4WD Trails: Southwest Colorado	$14.95		
4WD Trails: North-Central Colorado	$14.95		
4WD Trails: South-Central Colorado	$14.95		
4WD Adventures: Colorado	$28.95		

Shipping and handling $4 for the first book and $3 for each additional book. Colorado residents add 3% sales tax.

Sub Total _____

Tax _____

Shipping _____

Total _____

Send my order to:

NAME (PLEASE PRINT) _____

COMPANY _____

STREET ADDRESS _____

CITY / STATE / ZIP _____

TELEPHONE ( ) _____

Method of payment:

❑ Check or money order enclosed
❑ VISA   ❑ MasterCard   ❑ American Express

CARD NUMBER _____

EXPIRATION DATE _____

CARDHOLDER'S SIGNATURE _____